LEARN PYTHON
THE HARD WAY

Third Edition

 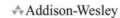

LEARN PYTHON
THE HARD WAY

A Very Simple Introduction
to the Terrifyingly Beautiful World
of Computers and Code

Third Edition

Zed A. Shaw

✦Addison-Wesley

Upper Saddle River, NJ • Boston • Indianapolis • San Francisco
New York • Toronto • Montreal • London • Munich • Paris • Madrid
Capetown • Sydney • Tokyo • Singapore • Mexico City

Many of the designations used by manufacturers and sellers to distinguish their products are claimed as trademarks. Where those designations appear in this book, and the publisher was aware of a trademark claim, the designations have been printed with initial capital letters or in all capitals.

The author and publisher have taken care in the preparation of this book, but make no expressed or implied warranty of any kind and assume no responsibility for errors or omissions. No liability is assumed for incidental or consequential damages in connection with or arising out of the use of the information or programs contained herein.

The publisher offers excellent discounts on this book when ordered in quantity for bulk purchases or special sales, which may include electronic versions and/or custom covers and content particular to your business, training goals, marketing focus, and branding interests. For more information, please contact:

U.S. Corporate and Government Sales
(800) 382-3419
corpsales@pearsontechgroup.com

For sales outside the United States, please contact:

International Sales
international@pearson.com

Visit us on the Web: informit.com/aw

Library of Congress Cataloging-in-Publication Data
Shaw, Zed.
  Learn Python the hard way : a very simple introduction to the terrifyingly beautiful world of computers and code / Zed A. Shaw.—Third edition.
     pages   cm
  Includes index.
  ISBN 978-0-321-88491-6 (paperback : alkaline paper)
  1. Python (Computer program language) 2. Python (Computer program language)—Problems, exercises, etc. 3. Computer programming—Problems, exercises, etc. I. Title.
  QA76.73.P98S53 2014
  005.13'3—dc23
                                                                        2013029738

ISBN-13: 978-0-321-88491-6
ISBN-10:   0-321-88491-4

Text printed in the United States on recycled paper at RR Donnelley in Crawfordsville, Indiana.
Seventh Printing, March 2015

Contents

Preface

This simple book is meant to get you started in programming. The title says it's the hard way to learn to write code, but it's actually not. It's only the "hard" way because it uses a technique called *instruction*. Instruction is where I tell you to do a sequence of controlled exercises designed to build a skill through repetition. This technique works very well with beginners who know nothing and need to acquire basic skills before they can understand more complex topics. It's used in everything from martial arts to music to even basic math and reading skills.

This book instructs you in Python by slowly building and establishing skills through techniques like practice and memorization, then applying them to increasingly difficult problems. By the end of the book, you will have the tools needed to begin learning more complex programming topics. I like to tell people that my book gives you your "programming black belt." What this means is that you know the basics well enough to now start *learning* programming.

If you work hard, take your time, and build these skills, you will learn to code.

Acknowledgments

I would like to thank Angela for helping me with the first two versions of this book. Without her, I probably wouldn't have bothered to finish it at all. She did the copy editing of the first draft and supported me immensely while I wrote it.

I'd also like to thank Greg Newman for doing the cover art for the first two editions, Brian Shumate for early website designs, and all the people who read previous editions of this book and took the time to send me feedback and corrections.

Thank you.

The Hard Way Is Easier

With the help of this book, you will do the incredibly simple things that all programmers do to learn a programming language:

1. Go through each exercise.

2. Type in each sample *exactly*.

3. Make it run.

That's it. This will be *very* difficult at first, but stick with it. If you go through this book and do each exercise for one or two hours a night, you will have a good foundation for moving on to another book. You might not really learn "programming" from this book, but you will learn the foundation skills you need to start learning the language.

This book's job is to teach you the three most essential skills that a beginning programmer needs to know: reading and writing, attention to detail, and spotting differences.

Reading and Writing

It seems stupidly obvious, but if you have a problem typing, you will have a problem learning to code. Especially if you have a problem typing the fairly odd characters in source code. Without this simple skill, you will be unable to learn even the most basic things about how software works.

Typing the code samples and getting them to run will help you learn the names of the symbols, get you familiar with typing them, and get you reading the language.

Attention to Detail

The one skill that separates bad programmers from good programmers is attention to detail. In fact, it's what separates the good from the bad in any profession. Without paying attention to the tiniest details of your work, you will miss key elements of what you create. In programming, this is how you end up with bugs and difficult-to-use systems.

By going through this book and copying each example *exactly*, you will be training your brain to focus on the details of what you are doing, as you are doing it.

Spotting Differences

A very important skill—which most programmers develop over time—is the ability to visually notice differences between things. An experienced programmer can take two pieces of code that are slightly different and immediately start pointing out the differences. Programmers have invented tools to make this even easier, but we won't be using any of these. You first have to train your brain the hard way—then you can use the tools.

While you do these exercises, typing each one in, you will make mistakes. It's inevitable; even seasoned programmers make a few. Your job is to compare what you have written to what's required and fix all the differences. By doing so, you will train yourself to notice mistakes, bugs, and other problems.

Do Not Copy-Paste

You must *type* each of these exercises in, manually. If you copy and paste, you might as well just not even do them. The point of these exercises is to train your hands, your brain, and your mind in how to read, write, and see code. If you copy-paste, you are cheating yourself out of the effectiveness of the lessons.

Using the Included Videos

Included in the third edition of *Learn Python The Hard Way* is more than five hours of instructional videos. There is one video for each exercise where I either demonstrate the exercise or give you tips for completing the exercise. The best way to use the videos is to attempt or complete the exercises without them first, then use the videos to review what you learned or if you are stuck. This will slowly wean you off of using videos to learn programming and will build your skills at understanding code directly. Stick with it, and over time you won't need these videos, or any videos, to learn programming. You'll be able to just read for the information you need.

A Word of Advice for "Visual Learners"

Your belief that you are "only" a visual learner is potentially holding you back in your educational goals. The idea that a person could only possibly learn from one of their senses is preposterous. It is possible to learn to use all of your senses when tackling a complex subject such as programming. If you've locked yourself in the visual- or kinetic-learner prison your whole life, then this book is a great way to break out of it and build up your analytic skills.

By first attempting each exercise from the book, you will build your skills at analytic thinking, skills which most likely you already have but have simply forgotten how to use effectively. However, when you get stuck, grab the video for that exercise and use your ability to process visual information to help. In fact, finding ways to apply all of your sense to a given difficult problem will give you new insights into that problem no matter how strange it may seem at first.

A Note on Practice and Persistence

While you are studying programming, I'm studying how to play guitar. I practice it every day for at least two hours a day. I play scales, chords, and arpeggios for an hour at least and then learn music theory, ear training, songs, and anything else I can. Some days I study guitar and music for eight hours because I feel like it and it's fun. To me, repetitive practice is natural and is just how to learn something. I know that to get good at anything you have to practice every day, even if I suck that day (which is often) or it's difficult. Keep trying and eventually it'll be easier and fun.

As you study this book and continue with programming, remember that anything worth doing is difficult at first. Maybe you are the kind of person who is afraid of failure, so you give up at the first sign of difficulty. Maybe you never learned self-discipline, so you can't do anything that's "boring." Maybe you were told that you are "gifted," so you never attempt anything that might make you seem stupid or not a prodigy. Maybe you are competitive and unfairly compare yourself to someone like me who's been programming for 20+ years.

Whatever your reason for wanting to quit, *keep at it*. Force yourself. If you run into a Study Drill you can't do or a lesson you just do not understand, then skip it and come back to it later. Just keep going because with programming there's this very odd thing that happens. At first, you will not understand anything. It'll be weird, just like with learning any human language. You will struggle with words and not know what symbols are what, and it'll all be very confusing. Then one day— *BANG*—your brain will snap and you will suddenly "get it." If you keep doing the exercises and keep trying to understand them, you will get it. You might not be a master coder, but you will at least understand how programming works.

If you give up, you won't ever reach this point. You will hit the first confusing thing (which is everything at first) and then stop. If you keep trying, keep typing it in, trying to understand it and reading about it, you will eventually get it.

But if you go through this whole book and you still do not understand how to code, at least you gave it a shot. You can say you tried your best and a little more and it didn't work out, but at least you tried. You can be proud of that.

A Warning for the Smarties

Sometimes people who already know a programming language will read this book and feel I'm insulting them. There is nothing in this book that is intended to be interpreted as condescending, insulting, or belittling. I simply know more about programming than my *intended* readers. If you think you are smarter than me, then you will feel talked down to and there's nothing I can do about that because you are not my *intended* reader.

If you are reading this book and flipping out at every third sentence because you feel I'm insulting your intelligence, then I have three points of advice for you:

1. Stop reading my book. I didn't write it for you. I wrote it for people who don't already know everything.

2. Empty before you fill. You will have a hard time learning from someone with more knowledge if you already know everything.

3. Go learn Lisp. I hear people who know everything really like Lisp.

For everyone else who's here to learn, just read everything as if I'm smiling and I have a mischievous little twinkle in my eye.

The Setup

This exercise has no code. It is simply the exercise you complete to get your computer to run Python. You should follow these instructions as exactly as possible. For example, Mac OSX computers already have Python 2, so do not install Python 3 (or any Python).

WARNING! If you do not know how to use PowerShell on Windows or the Terminal on OSX or "Bash" on Linux, then you need to go learn that first. I have included an abbreviated version of my book *The Command Line Crash Course* in the appendix. Go through that first and then come back to these instructions.

Mac OSX

To complete this exercise, complete the following tasks:

1. Go to http://www.barebones.com/products/textwrangler with your browser, get the TextWrangler text editor, and install it.

2. Put TextWrangler (your editor) in your dock so you can reach it easily.

3. Find your Terminal program. Search for it. You will find it.

4. Put your Terminal in your dock as well.

5. Run your Terminal program. It won't look like much.

6. In your Terminal program, run python. You run things in Terminal by just typing the name and hitting RETURN.

7. Hit CTRL-Z (^Z), Enter, and get out of python.

8. You should be back at a prompt similar to what you had before you typed python. If not, find out why.

9. Learn how to make a directory in the Terminal.

10. Learn how to change into a directory in the Terminal.

11. Use your editor to create a file in this directory. You will make the file, "Save" or "Save As . . . ," and pick this directory.

12. Go back to Terminal using just the keyboard to switch windows.

13. Back in Terminal, see if you can list the directory to see your newly created file.

OSX: What You Should See

Here's me doing this on my computer in Terminal. Your computer would be different, so see if you can figure out all the differences between what I did and what you should do.

```
Last login: Sat Apr 24 00:56:54 on ttys001
~ $ python
Python 2.5.1 (r251:54863, Feb  6 2009, 19:02:12)
[GCC 4.0.1 (Apple Inc. build 5465)] on darwin
Type "help", "copyright", "credits" or "license" for more information.
>>> ^D
~ $ mkdir mystuff
~ $ cd mystuff
mystuff $ ls
# ... Use TextWrangler here to edit test.txt....
mystuff $ ls
test.txt
mystuff $
```

[handwritten annotation: QUIT CTRL →D (MAC)]

Windows

1. Go to http://notepad-plus-plus.org with your browser, get the Notepad++ text editor, and install it. You do not need to be the administrator to do this.

2. Make sure you can get to Notepad++ easily by putting it on your desktop and/or in Quick Launch. Both options are available during setup.

3. Run PowerShell from the Start menu. Search for it and you can just hit Enter to run it.

4. Make a shortcut to it on your desktop and/or Quick Launch for your convenience.

5. Run your Terminal program. It won't look like much.

6. In your Terminal program, run python. You run things in Terminal by just typing the name and hitting Enter.
    a. If you run python and it's not there (python is not recognized.), install it from http://python.org/download.
    b. *Make sure you install Python 2, not Python 3.*
    c. You may be better off with ActiveState Python, especially if you do not have administrative rights.
    d. If after you install it python still isn't recognized, then in PowerShell enter this:

    ```
    [Environment]::SetEnvironmentVariable("Path", "$env:Path;C:\Python27", "User")
    ```

    e. Close PowerShell and then start it again to make sure Python now runs. If it doesn't, restart may be required.

7. Type quit() and hit Enter to exit python.

8. You should be back at a prompt similar to what you had before you typed python. If not, find out why.

9. Learn how to make a directory in the Terminal.

10. Learn how to change into a directory in the Terminal.

11. Use your editor to create a file in this directory. Make the file, Save or Save As... and pick this directory.

12. Go back to Terminal using just the keyboard to switch windows.

13. Back in Terminal, see if you can list the directory to see your newly created file.

WARNING! If you missed it, sometimes you install Python on Windows and it doesn't configure the path correctly. Make sure you enter [Environment]::SetEnvironment Variable("Path", "$env:Path;C:\Python27", "User") in PowerShell to configure it correctly. You also have to either restart PowerShell or restart your whole computer to get it to really be fixed.

Windows: What You Should See

```
> python
ActivePython 2.6.5.12 (ActiveState Software Inc.) based on
Python 2.6.5 (r265:79063, Mar 20 2010, 14:22:52) [MSC v.1500 32 bit (Intel)] on win32
Type "help", "copyright", "credits" or "license" for more information.
>>> ^Z


> mkdir mystuff

> cd mystuff

... Here you would use Notepad++ to make test.txt in mystuff ...

>
 <bunch of unimportant errors if you installed it as non-admin - ignore them - hit Enter>
> dir
Volume in drive C is
Volume Serial Number is 085C-7E02

Directory of C:\Documents and Settings\you\mystuff

04.05.2010  23:32    <DIR>          .
04.05.2010  23:32    <DIR>          ..
04.05.2010  23:32                 6 test.txt
```

```
                1 File(s)              6 bytes
                2 Dir(s)   14 804 623 360 bytes free


        >
```

You will probably see a very different prompt, Python information, and other stuff, but this is the general idea.

Linux

Linux is a varied operating system with a bunch of different ways to install software. I'm assuming if you are running Linux then you know how to install packages, so here are your instructions:

1. Use your Linux package manager and install the gedit text editor.

2. Make sure you can get to gedit easily by putting it in your window manager's menu.
    a. Run gedit so we can fix some stupid defaults it has.
    b. Open Preferences and select the Editor tab.
    c. Change Tab width: to 4.
    d. Select (make sure a check mark is in) Insert spaces instead of tabs.
    e. Turn on Automatic indentation as well.
    f. Open the View tab and turn on Display line numbers.

3. Find your Terminal program. It could be called GNOME Terminal, Konsole, or xterm.

4. Put your Terminal in your dock as well.

5. Run your Terminal program. It won't look like much.

6. In your Terminal program, run Python. You run things in Terminal by just typing the name and hitting Enter.
    a. If you run Python and it's not there, install it. *Make sure you install Python 2, not Python 3.*

7. Type quit() and hit Enter to exit Python.

8. You should be back at a prompt similar to what you had before you typed python. If not, find out why.

9. Learn how to make a directory in the Terminal.

10. Learn how to change into a directory in the Terminal.

11. Use your editor to create a file in this directory. Typically you will make the file, Save or Save As . . ., and pick this directory.

12. Go back to Terminal using just the keyboard to switch windows. Look it up if you can't figure it out.

13. Back in Terminal, see if you can list the directory to see your newly created file.

Linux: What You Should See

```
$ python
Python 2.6.5 (r265:79063, Apr  1 2010, 05:28:39)
[GCC 4.4.3 20100316 (prerelease)] on linux2
Type "help", "copyright", "credits" or "license" for more information.
>>>
$ mkdir mystuff
$ cd mystuff
# ... Use gedit here to edit test.txt ...
$ ls
test.txt
$
```

You will probably see a very different prompt, Python information, and other stuff, but this is the general idea.

Warnings for Beginners

You are done with this exercise. This exercise might be hard for you, depending on your familiarity with your computer. If it is difficult, take the time to read and study and get through it, because until you can do these very basic things, you will find it difficult to get much programming done.

If a programmer tells you to use vim or emacs, just say "no." These editors are for when you are a better programmer. All you need right now is an editor that lets you put text into a file. We will use gedit, TextWrangler, or Notepad++ (from now on called "the text editor" or "a text editor") because it is simple and the same on all computers. Professional programmers use these text editors, so it's good enough for you starting out.

A programmer may try to get you to install Python 3 and learn that. Say, "When all the Python code on your computer is Python 3, then I'll try to learn it." That should keep him or her busy for about 10 years.

A programmer will eventually tell you to use Mac OSX or Linux. If the programmer likes fonts and typography, he'll tell you to get a Mac OSX computer. If he likes control and has a huge beard, he'll tell you to install Linux. Again, use whatever computer you have right now that works. All you need is an editor, a Terminal, and Python.

Finally, the purpose of this setup is so you can do four things very reliably while you work on the exercises:

1. *Write* exercises using your text editor, gedit on Linux, TextWrangler on OSX, or Notepad++ on Windows.

2. *Run* the exercises you wrote.

3. *Fix* them when they are broken.

4. Repeat.

Anything else will only confuse you, so stick to the plan.

A Good First Program

Remember, you should have spent a good amount of time in Exercise 0, learning how to install a text editor, run the text editor, run the Terminal, and work with both of them. If you haven't done that, then do not go on. You will not have a good time. This is the only time I'll start an exercise with a warning that you should not skip or get ahead of yourself.

Type the following text into a single file named ex1.py. This is important, as Python works best with files ending in .py.

ex1.py

```
1    print "Hello World!"
2    print "Hello Again"
3    print "I like typing this."
4    print "This is fun."
5    print 'Yay! Printing.'
6    print "I'd much rather you 'not'."
7    print 'I "said" do not touch this.'
```

If you are on Mac OSX, then this is what your text editor might look like if you use TextWrangler:

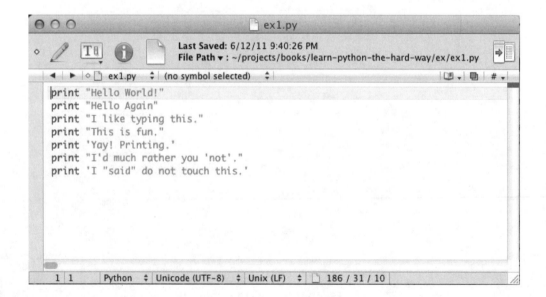

If you are on Windows using Notepad++, then this is what it would look like:

```
C:\Users\zed\lpthw\ex1.py - Notepad++

File  Edit  Search  View  Encoding  Language  Settings  Macro  Run  Plugins  Window  ?                    X

ex1.py

  1    print "Hello World!"
  2    print "Hello Again"
  3    print "I like typing this."
  4    print "This is fun."
  5    print 'Yay! Printing.'
  6    print "I'd much rather you 'not'."
  7    print 'I "said" do not touch this.'
  8
  9

Pytl length : 193   lines : 9          Ln : 1  Col : 1  Sel : 0            Dos\Windows       ANSI              INS
```

Don't worry if your editor doesn't look exactly the same; the key points are as follows:

1. Notice I did not type the line numbers on the left. Those are printed in the book so I can talk about specific lines by saying, "See line 5 . . ." You do not type those into Python scripts.

2. Notice I have the `print` at the beginning of the line and how it looks exactly the same as what I have above. Exactly means exactly, not kind of sort of the same. Every single character has to match for it to work. But the colors are all different. Color doesn't matter; only the characters you type.

Then in Terminal, *run* the file by typing:

```
python ex1.py
```

If you did it right, then you should see the same output I have below. If not, you have done something wrong. No, the computer is not wrong.

What You Should See

On Max OSX in the Terminal, you should see this:

```
zedshaw$ python ex1.py
Hello World!
Hello Again
I like typing this.
This is fun.
Yay! Printing.
I'd much rather you 'not'.
I "said" do not touch this.
zedshaw$
```

On Windows in PowerShell, you should see this:

```
PS C:\Users\zed\lpthw> python ex1.py
Hello World!
Hello Again
I like typing this.
This is fun.
Yay! Printing.
I'd much rather you 'not'.
I "said" do not touch this.
PS C:\Users\zed\lpthw>
```

You may see different names, the name of your computer or other things, before the python ex1.py, but the important part is that you type the command and see the output is the same as mine.

If you have an error, it will look like this:

```
$ python ex/ex1.py
  File "ex/ex1.py", line 3
    print "I like typing this.
                              ^
SyntaxError: EOL while scanning string literal
```

It's important that you can read these, since you will be making many of these mistakes. Even I make many of these mistakes. Let's look at this line by line.

1. Here we ran our command in the Terminal to run the ex1.py script.

2. Python then tells us that the file ex1.py has an error on line 3.

3. It then prints this line for us.

4. Then it puts a ∧ (caret) character to point at where the problem is. Notice the missing " (double-quote) character?

5. Finally, it prints out a SyntaxError and tells us something about what might be the error. Usually these are very cryptic, but if you copy that text into a search engine, you will find someone else who's had that error and you can probably figure out how to fix it.

WARNING! If you are from another country and you get errors about ASCII encodings, then put this at the top of your Python scripts:

```
# -*- coding: utf-8 -*-
```

It will fix them so that you can use Unicode UTF-8 in your scripts without a problem.

Study Drills

Each exercise also contains Study Drills. The Study Drills contain things you should *try* to do. If you can't, skip it and come back later.

For this exercise, try these things:

1. Make your script print another line.

2. Make your script print only one of the lines.

3. Put a "#" (octothorpe) character at the beginning of a line. What did it do? Try to find out what this character does.

From now on, I won't explain how each exercise works unless an exercise is different.

NOTE: An "octothorpe" is also called a "pound," "hash," "mesh," or any number of names. Pick the one that makes you chill out.

Common Student Questions

These are *actual* questions by real students in the comments section of the book when it was online. You may run into some of these, so I've collected and answered them for you.

Can I use IDLE?
No, you should use Terminal on OSX and PowerShell on Windows, just like I have here. If you don't know how to use those, then you can go read the Command Line Crash Course in the appendix.

How do you get colors in your editor?
Save your file first as a `.py` file, such as `ex1.py`. Then you'll have color when you type.

I get SyntaxError: invalid syntax when I run ex1.py.
You are probably trying to run Python, then trying to type Python again. Close your Terminal, start it again, and right away type only `python ex1.py`.

I get can't open file 'ex1.py': [Errno 2] No such file or directory.
You need to be in the same directory as the file you created. Make sure you use the `cd` command to go there first. For example, if you saved your file in `lpthw/ex1.py`, then you would do `cd lpthw/` before trying to run `python ex1.py`. If you don't know what any of that means, then go through the Command Line Crash Course (CLI-CC) mentioned in the first question.

How do I get my country's language characters into my file?
Make sure you type this at the top of your file: `# -*- coding: utf-8 -*-`.

My file doesn't run; I just get the prompt back with no output.
You most likely took the previous code literally and thought that `print "Hello World!"` meant to literally print just `"Hello World!"` into the file, without the `print`. Your file has to be *exactly* like mine in the previous code and all the screenshots; I have `print "Hello World!"` and `print` before every line. Make sure your code is like mine and it should work.

Comments and Pound Characters

Comments are very important in your programs. They are used to tell you what something does in English, and they also are used to disable parts of your program if you need to remove them temporarily. Here's how you use comments in Python:

ex2.py

```
1    # A comment, this is so you can read your program later.
2    # Anything after the # is ignored by python.
3
4    print "I could have code like this." # and the comment after is ignored
5
6    # You can also use a comment to "disable" or comment out a piece of code:
7    # print "This won't run."
8
9    print "This will run."
```

From now on, I'm going to write code like this. It is important for you to understand that everything does not have to be literal. Your screen and program may visually look different, but what's important is the text you type into the file you're writing in your text editor. In fact, I could work with any text editor and the results would be the same.

What You Should See

Exercise 2 Session

```
$ python ex2.py
I could have code like this.
This will run.
```

Again, I'm not going to show you screenshots of all the Terminals possible. You should understand that the above is not a literal translation of what your output should look like visually, but the text between the first $ Python ... and last $ lines will be what you focus on.

Study Drills

1. Find out if you were right about what the # character does and make sure you know what it's called (octothorpe or pound character).

2. Take your ex2.py file and review each line going backward. Start at the last line, and check each word in reverse against what you should have typed.

3.   Did you find more mistakes? Fix them.

4.   Read what you typed previously out loud, including saying each character by its name. Did you find more mistakes? Fix them.

Common Student Questions

Are you sure # is called the pound character?
I call it the octothorpe and that is the only name that no country uses and that works in every country. Every country thinks its way to call this one character is both the most important way to do it and also the only way it's done. To me this is simply arrogance and, really, y'all should just chill out and focus on more important things like learning to code.

If # is for comments, then how come # -*- coding: utf-8 -*- works?
Python still ignores that as code, but it's used as a kind of "hack" or workaround for problems with setting and detecting the format of a file. You also find a similar kind of comment for editor settings.

Why does the # in print "Hi # there." not get ignored?
The # in that code is inside a string, so it will be put into the string until the ending " character is hit. These pound characters are just considered characters and aren't considered comments.

How do I comment out multiple lines?
Put a # in front of each one.

I can't figure out how to type a # character on my country's keyboard?
Some countries use the Alt key and combinations of those to print characters foreign to their language. You'll have to look online in a search engine to see how to type it.

Why do I have to read code backward?
It's a trick to make your brain not attach meaning to each part of the code, and doing that makes you process each piece exactly. This catches errors and is a handy error-checking technique.

Numbers and Math

Every programming language has some kind of way of doing numbers and math. Do not worry: programmers lie frequently about being math geniuses when they really aren't. If they were math geniuses, they would be doing math, not writing ads and social network games to steal people's money.

This exercise has lots of math symbols. Let's name them right away so you know what they are called. As you type this one in, say the names. When saying them feels boring, you can stop saying them. Here are the names:

+   plus

−   minus

/   slash

*   asterisk

%   percent

<   less-than

>   greater-than

<= less-than-equal

>= greater-than-equal

Notice how the operations are missing? After you type in the code for this exercise, go back and figure out what each of these does and complete the table. For example, + does addition.

ex3.py

```
1    print "I will now count my chickens:"
2
3    print "Hens", 25 + 30 / 6
4    print "Roosters", 100 - 25 * 3 % 4
5
6    print "Now I will count the eggs:"
7
8    print 3 + 2 + 1 - 5 + 4 % 2 - 1 / 4 + 6
9
10   print "Is it true that 3 + 2 < 5 - 7?"
11
12   print 3 + 2 < 5 - 7
13
14   print "What is 3 + 2?", 3 + 2
```

```
15   print "What is 5 - 7?", 5 - 7
16
17   print "Oh, that's why it's False."
18
19   print "How about some more."
20
21   print "Is it greater?", 5 > -2
22   print "Is it greater or equal?", 5 >= -2
23   print "Is it less or equal?", 5 <= -2
```

What You Should See

```
$ python ex3.py
I will now count my chickens:
Hens 30
Roosters 97
Now I will count the eggs:
7
Is it true that 3 + 2 < 5 - 7?
False
What is 3 + 2? 5
What is 5 - 7? -2
Oh, that's why it's False.
How about some more.
Is it greater? True
Is it greater or equal? True
Is it less or equal? False
```

Study Drills

1. Above each line, use the # to write a comment to yourself explaining what the line does.

2. Remember in Exercise 0 when you started Python? Start Python this way again and, using the above characters and what you know, use Python as a calculator.

3. Find something you need to calculate and write a new .py file that does it.

4. Notice the math seems "wrong"? There are no fractions, only whole numbers. Find out why by researching what a "floating point" number is.

5. Rewrite ex3.py to use floating point numbers so it's more accurate (hint: 20.0 is floating point).

Common Student Questions

Why is the % character a "modulus" and not a "percent"?
Mostly that's just how the designers chose to use that symbol. In normal writing, you are correct to read it as a "percent." In programming, this calculation is typically done with simple division and the / operator. The % modulus is a different operation that just happens to use the % symbol.

How does % work?
Another way to say it is "X divided by Y with J remaining." For example, "100 divided by 16 with 4 remaining." The result of % is the J part, or the remaining part.

What is the order of operations?
In the United States we use an acronym called PEMDAS, which stands for Parentheses Exponents Multiplication Division Addition Subtraction. That's the order Python follows as well.

Why does / (divide) round down?
It's not really rounding down; it's just dropping the fractional part after the decimal. Try doing 7.0 / 4.0 and compare it to 7 / 4 and you'll see the difference.

Variables and Names

Now you can print things with print and you can do math. The next step is to learn about variables. In programming, a variable is nothing more than a name for something so you can use the name rather than the something as you code. Programmers use these variable names to make their code read more like English and because they have lousy memories. If they didn't use good names for things in their software, they'd get lost when they tried to read their code again.

If you get stuck with this exercise, remember the tricks you have been taught so far of finding differences and focusing on details:

1. Write a comment above each line explaining to yourself what it does in English.

2. Read your .py file backward.

3. Read your .py file out loud, saying even the characters.

ex4.py

```
1    cars = 100
2    space_in_a_car = 4.0
3    drivers = 30
4    passengers = 90
5    cars_not_driven = cars - drivers
6    cars_driven = drivers
7    carpool_capacity = cars_driven * space_in_a_car
8    average_passengers_per_car = passengers / cars_driven
9
10
11   print "There are", cars, "cars available."
12   print "There are only", drivers, "drivers available."
13   print "There will be", cars_not_driven, "empty cars today."
14   print "We can transport", carpool_capacity, "people today."
15   print "We have", passengers, "to carpool today."
16   print "We need to put about", average_passengers_per_car, "in each car."
```

NOTE: The _ in space_in_a_car is called an underscore character. Find out how to type it if you do not already know. We use this character a lot to put an imaginary space between words in variable names.

What You Should See

```
$ python ex4.py
There are 100 cars available.
There are only 30 drivers available.
There will be 70 empty cars today.
We can transport 120.0 people today.
We have 90 to carpool today.
We need to put about 3 in each car.
```

Study Drills

When I wrote this program the first time I had a mistake, and Python told me about it like this:

```
Traceback (most recent call last):
    File "ex4.py", line 8, in <module>
      average_passengers_per_car = car_pool_capacity / passenger
  NameError: name 'car_pool_capacity' is not defined
```

Explain this error in your own words. Make sure you use line numbers and explain why.

Here's more Study Drills:

1. I used 4.0 for space_in_a_car, but is that necessary? What happens if it's just 4?

2. Remember that 4.0 is a "floating point" number. Find out what that means.

3. Write comments above each of the variable assignments.

4. Make sure you know what = is called (equals) and that it's making names for things.

5. Remember that _ is an underscore character.

6. Try running Python as a calculator like you did before and use variable names to do your calculations. Popular variable names are also i, x, and j.

Common Student Questions

What is the difference between = (single-equal) and == (double-equal)?
The = (single-equal) assigns the value on the right to a variable on the left. The == (double-equal) tests if two things have the same value, and you'll learn about this in Exercise 27.

Can we write x=100 instead of x = 100?
You can, but it's bad form. You should add space around operators like this so that it's easier to read.

How can I print without spaces between words in `print`?
You do it like this: `print "Hey %s there." % "you"`. You will do more of this soon.

What do you mean by "read the file backward"?
Very simple. Imagine you have a file with 16 lines of code in it. Start at line 16, and compare it to my file at line 16. Then do it again for 15, and so on, until you've read the whole file backward.

Why did you use `4.0` for space?
It is mostly so you can then find out what a floating point number is and ask this question. See the Study Drills.

More Variables and Printing

Now we'll do even more typing of variables and printing them out. This time we'll use something called a "format string." Every time you put " (double-quotes) around a piece of text, you have been making a *string*. A string is how you make something that your program might give to a human. You print them, save them to files, send them to web servers, all sorts of things.

Strings are really handy, so in this exercise you will learn how to make strings that have variables embedded in them. You embed variables inside a string by using specialized format sequences and then putting the variables at the end with a special syntax that tells Python, "Hey, this is a format string, put these variables in there."

As usual, just type this in even if you do not understand it and make it exactly the same.

ex5.py

```
1    my_name = 'Zed A. Shaw'
2    my_age = 35 # not a lie
3    my_height = 74 # inches
4    my_weight = 180 # lbs
5    my_eyes = 'Blue'
6    my_teeth = 'White'
7    my_hair = 'Brown'
8
9    print "Let's talk about %s." % my_name
10   print "He's %d inches tall." % my_height
11   print "He's %d pounds heavy." % my_weight
12   print "Actually that's not too heavy."
13   print "He's got %s eyes and %s hair." % (my_eyes, my_hair)
14   print "His teeth are usually %s depending on the coffee." % my_teeth
15
16   # this line is tricky, try to get it exactly right
17   print "If I add %d, %d, and %d I get %d." % (
18       my_age, my_height, my_weight, my_age + my_height + my_weight)
```

WARNING! Remember to put # -- coding: utf-8 -- at the top if you use non-ASCII characters and get an encoding error.

What You Should See

Exercise 5 Session

```
$ python ex5.py
Let's talk about Zed A. Shaw.
He's 74 inches tall.
```

He's 180 pounds heavy.
Actually that's not too heavy.
He's got Blue eyes and Brown hair.
His teeth are usually White depending on the coffee.
If I add 35, 74, and 180 I get 289.

Study Drills

1. Change all the variables so there isn't the my_ in front. Make sure you change the name everywhere, not just where you used = to set them.

2. Try more format characters. %r is a very useful one. It's like saying "print this no matter what."

3. Search online for all the Python format characters.

4. Try to write some variables that convert the inches and pounds to centimeters and kilos. Do not just type in the measurements. Work out the math in Python.

Common Student Questions

Can I make a variable like this: 1 = 'Zed Shaw'?
No, the 1 is not a valid variable name. They need to start with a character, so a1 would work, but 1 will not.

What does %s, %r, and %d do again?
You'll learn more about this as you continue, but they are "formatters." They tell Python to take the variable on the right and put it in to replace the %s with its value.

I don't get it, what is a "formatter"? Huh?
The problem with teaching you programming is that to understand many of my descriptions, you need to know how to do programming already. The way I solve this is I make you do something, and then I explain it later. When you run into these kinds of questions, write them down and see if I explain it later.

How can I round a floating point number?
You can use the **round()** function like this: **round(1.7333)**.

I get this error TypeError: 'str' object is not callable.
You probably forgot the % between the string and the list of variables.

Why does this not make sense to me?
Try making the numbers in this script your measurements. It's weird, but talking about yourself will make it seem more real.

Strings and Text

While you have already been writing strings, you still do not know what they do. In this exercise, we create a bunch of variables with complex strings so you can see what they are for. First an explanation of strings.

A string is usually a bit of text you want to display to someone or "export" out of the program you are writing. Python knows you want something to be a string when you put either " (double-quotes) or ' (single-quotes) around the text. You saw this many times with your use of print when you put the text you want to go to the string inside " or ' after the print. Then Python prints it.

Strings may contain the format characters you have discovered so far. You simply put the formatted variables in the string, and then a % (percent) character, followed by the variable. The *only* catch is that if you want multiple formats in your string to print multiple variables, you need to put them inside ( ) (parentheses) separated by , (commas). It's as if you were telling me to buy you a list of items from the store and you said, "I want milk, eggs, bread, and soup." Only as a programmer we say, "(milk, eggs, bread, soup)."

We will now type in a whole bunch of strings, variables, and formats, and print them. You will also practice using short abbreviated variable names. Programmers love saving themselves time at your expense by using annoying cryptic variable names, so let's get you started being able to read and write them early on.

ex6.py

```
1    x = "There are %d types of people." % 10
2    binary = "binary"
3    do_not = "don't"
4    y = "Those who know %s and those who %s." % (binary, do_not)
5
6    print x
7    print y
8
9    print "I said: %r." % x
10   print "I also said: '%s'." % y
11
12   hilarious = False
13   joke_evaluation = "Isn't that joke so funny?! %r"
14
15   print joke_evaluation % hilarious
16
17   w = "This is the left side of..."
18   e = "a string with a right side."
19
20   print w + e
```

What You Should See

```
$ python ex6.py
There are 10 types of people.
Those who know binary and those who don't.
I said: 'There are 10 types of people.'.
I also said: 'Those who know binary and those who don't.'.
Isn't that joke so funny?! False
This is the left side of...a string with a right side.
```

Study Drills

1. Go through this program and write a comment above each line explaining it.

2. Find all the places where a string is put inside a string. There are four places.

3. Are you sure there are only four places? How do you know? Maybe I like lying.

4. Explain why adding the two strings w and e with + makes a longer string.

Common Student Questions

What is the difference between %r and %s?
We use %r for debugging, since it displays the "raw" data of the variable, but we use %s and others for displaying to users.

What's the point of %s and %d when you can just use %r?
The %r is best for debugging, and the other formats are for actually displaying variables to users.

If you thought the joke was funny could you write `hilarious = True`?
Yes, and you'll learn more about these boolean values in Exercise 27.

Why do you put ' (single-quotes) around some strings and not others?
Mostly it's because of style, but I'll use a single-quote inside a string that has double-quotes. Look at line 10 to see how I'm doing that.

I get the error `TypeError: not all arguments converted during string formatting`.
You need to make sure that the line of code is exactly the same. What happens in this error is you have more % format characters in the string than variables to put in them. Go back and figure out what you did wrong.

More Printing

Now we are going to do a bunch of exercises where you just type code in and make it run. I won't be explaining much since it is just more of the same. The purpose is to build up your chops. See you in a few exercises, and *do not skip!* Do not *paste!*

ex7.py

```
1    print "Mary had a little lamb."
2    print "Its fleece was white as %s." % 'snow'
3    print "And everywhere that Mary went."
4    print "." * 10   # what'd that do?
5
6    end1 = "C"
7    end2 = "h"
8    end3 = "e"
9    end4 = "e"
10   end5 = "s"
11   end6 = "e"
12   end7 = "B"
13   end8 = "u"
14   end9 = "r"
15   end10 = "g"
16   end11 = "e"
17   end12 = "r"
18
19   # watch that comma at the end.  try removing it to see what happens
20   print end1 + end2 + end3 + end4 + end5 + end6,
21   print end7 + end8 + end9 + end10 + end11 + end12
```

What You Should See

Exercise 7 Session

```
$ python ex7.py
Mary had a little lamb.
Its fleece was white as snow.
And everywhere that Mary went.
..........
Cheese Burger
```

Study Drills

For these next few exercises, you will have the exact same Study Drills.

1. Go back through and write a comment on what each line does.

2. Read each one backward or out loud to find your errors.

3. From now on, when you make mistakes, write down on a piece of paper what kind of mistake you made.

4. When you go to the next exercise, look at the last mistakes you made and try not to make them in this new one.

5. Remember that everyone makes mistakes. Programmers are like magicians who like everyone to think they are perfect and never wrong, but it's all an act. They make mistakes all the time.

Common Student Questions

How does the "end" statement work?
These are not really an "end statement," but actually the names of variables that just happen to have the word "end" in them.

Why are you using the variable named 'snow'?
That's actually not a variable: it is just a string with the word snow in it. A variable wouldn't have the single-quotes around it.

Is it normal to write an English comment for every line of code like you say to do in Study Drills #1?
No, normally you write comments only to explain difficult to understand code or why you did something. Why (or your motivation) is usually much more important, and then you try to write the code so that it explains how something is being done on its own. However, sometimes you just have to write such nasty code to solve a problem that it does need a comment on every line. In this case, though, it's strictly for you to get better at translating from code to English.

Can I use single-quotes or double-quotes to make a string or do they do different things?
In Python either way to make a string is acceptable, although typically you'll use single-quotes for any short strings like 'a' or 'snow'.

Couldn't you just not use the comma , and turn the last two lines into one single-line print?
Yes, you could very easily, but then it'd be longer than 80 characters, which in Python is bad style.

Printing, Printing

ex8.py

```
1    formatter = "%r %r %r %r"
2
3    print formatter % (1, 2, 3, 4)
4    print formatter % ("one", "two", "three", "four")
5    print formatter % (True, False, False, True)
6    print formatter % (formatter, formatter, formatter, formatter)
7    print formatter % (
8        "I had this thing.",
9        "That you could type up right.",
10       "But it didn't sing.",
11       "So I said goodnight."
12   )
```

What You Should See

Exercise 8 Session

```
$ python ex8.py
1 2 3 4
'one' 'two' 'three' 'four'
True False False True
'%r %r %r %r' '%r %r %r %r' '%r %r %r %r' '%r %r %r %r'
'I had this thing.' 'That you could type up right.' "But it didn't sing."
'So I said goodnight.'
```

Study Drills

1. Do your checks of your work, write down your mistakes, and try not to make them on the next exercise.

2. Notice that the last line of output uses both single-quotes and double-quotes for individual pieces. Why do you think that is?

Common Student Questions

Should I use %s or %r for formatting?
You should use %s and only use %r for getting debugging information about something. The %r will give you the "raw programmer's" version of variable, also known as the "representation."

Why do I have to put quotes around "one" but not around True or False?

That's because Python recognizes True and False as keywords representing the concept of true and false. If you put quotes around them, then they are turned into strings and won't work right. You'll learn more about how these work in Exercise 27.

I tried putting Chinese (or some other non-ASCII characters) into these strings, but %r prints out weird symbols.

Use %s to print that instead and it'll work.

Why does %r sometimes print things with single-quotes when I wrote them with double-quotes?

Python is going to print the strings in the most efficient way it can, not replicate exactly the way you wrote them. This is perfectly fine since %r is used for debugging and inspection, so it's not necessary that it be pretty.

Why doesn't this work in Python 3?

Don't use Python 3. Use Python 2.7 or better, although Python 2.6 might work fine.

Can I use IDLE to run this?

No, you should learn to use the command line. It is essential to learning programming and is a good place to start if you want to learn about programming. IDLE will fail for you when you get further in the book.

Printing, Printing, Printing

ex9.py

```
1    # Here's some new strange stuff, remember type it exactly.
2
3    days = "Mon Tue Wed Thu Fri Sat Sun"
4    months = "Jan\nFeb\nMar\nApr\nMay\nJun\nJul\nAug"
5
6    print "Here are the days: ", days
7    print "Here are the months: ", months
8
9    print """
10   There's something going on here.
11   With the three double-quotes.
12   We'll be able to type as much as we like.
13   Even 4 lines if we want, or 5, or 6.
14   """
```

What You Should See

Exercise 9 Session

```
$ python ex9.py
Here are the days:  Mon Tue Wed Thu Fri Sat Sun
Here are the months:  Jan
Feb
Mar
Apr
May
Jun
Jul
Aug

There's something going on here.
With the three double-quotes.
We'll be able to type as much as we like.
Even 4 lines if we want, or 5, or 6.
```

Study Drills

1. Do your checks of your work, write down your mistakes, and try not to make them on the next exercise.

Common Student Questions

What if I wanted to start the months on a new line?
You simply start the string with \n like this:

```
"\nJan\nFeb\nMar\nApr\nMay\nJun\nJul\nAug"
```

Why do the \n newlines not work when I use %r?
That's how %r formatting works; it prints it the way you wrote it (or close to it). It's the "raw" format for debugging.

Why do I get an error when I put spaces between the three double-quotes?
You have to type them like """ and not " " ", meaning with *no* spaces between each one.

Is it bad that my errors are always spelling mistakes?
Most programming errors in the beginning (and even later) are simple spelling mistakes, typos, or getting simple things out of order.

What Was That?

In Exercise 9 I threw you some new stuff, just to keep you on your toes. I showed you two ways to make a string that goes across multiple lines. In the first way, I put the characters \n (backslash n) between the names of the months. What these two characters do is put a new line character into the string at that point.

This use of the \ (backslash) character is a way we can put difficult-to-type characters into a string. There are plenty of these "escape sequences" available for different characters you might want to put in, but there's a special one, the double backslash, which is just two of them \. These two characters will print just one backslash. We'll try a few of these sequences so you can see what I mean.

Another important escape sequence is to escape a single-quote ' or double-quote ". Imagine you have a string that uses double-quotes and you want to put a double-quote in for the output. If you do this "I "understand" joe." then Python will get confused since it will think the " around "understand" actually *ends* the string. You need a way to tell Python that the " inside the string isn't a *real* double-quote.

To solve this problem, you *escape* double-quotes and single-quotes so Python knows what to include in the string. Here's an example:

```
"I am 6'2\" tall."  # escape double-quote inside string
'I am 6\'2" tall.'  # escape single-quote inside string
```

The second way is by using triple-quotes, which is just """ and works like a string, but you also can put as many lines of text as you want until you type """ again. We'll also play with these.

ex10.py

```
1    tabby_cat = "\tI'm tabbed in."
2    persian_cat = "I'm split\non a line."
3    backslash_cat = "I'm \\ a \\ cat."
4
5    fat_cat = """
6    I'll do a list:
7    \t* Cat food
8    \t* Fishies
9    \t* Catnip\n\t* Grass
10   """
11
12   print tabby_cat
13   print persian_cat
14   print backslash_cat
15   print fat_cat
```

What You Should See

Look for the tab characters that you made. In this exercise, the spacing is important to get right.

```
$ python ex10.py
        I'm tabbed in.
I'm split
on a line.
I'm \ a \ cat.

I'll do a list:
        * Cat food
        * Fishies
        * Catnip
        * Grass
```

Escape Sequences

This is the list of all the escape sequences Python supports. You may not use many of these, but memorize their format and what they do anyway. Also try them out in some strings to see if you can make them work.

Escape	What it does.
\\	Backslash (\)
\'	Single-quote (')
\"	Double-quote (")
\a	ASCII bell (BEL)
\b	ASCII backspace (BS)
\f	ASCII formfeed (FF)
\n	ASCII linefeed (LF)
\N{name}	Character named name in the Unicode database (Unicode only)
\r	ASCII carriage return (CR)
\t	ASCII horizontal tab (TAB)
\uxxxx	Character with 16-bit hex value xxxx (Unicode only)
\Uxxxxxxxx	Character with 32-bit hex value xxxxxxxx (Unicode only)
\v	ASCII vertical tab (VT)
\ooo	Character with octal value oo
\xhh	Character with hex value hh

Here's a tiny piece of fun code to try out:

```
while True:
    for i in ["/","-","|","\\","|"]:
        print "%s\r" % i,
```

Study Drills

1. Memorize all the escape sequences by putting them on flash cards.

2. Use ''' (triple-single-quote) instead. Can you see why you might use that instead of """?

3. Combine escape sequences and format strings to create a more complex format.

4. Remember the %r format? Combine %r with double-quote and single-quote escapes and print them out. Compare %r with %s. Notice how %r prints it the way you'd write it in your file, but %s prints it the way you'd like to see it?

Common Student Questions

I still haven't completely figured out the last exercise. Should I continue?
Yes, keep going, and instead of stopping, take notes listing things you don't understand for each exercise. Periodically go through your notes and see if you can figure these things out after you've completed more exercises. Sometimes, though, you may need to go back a few exercises and go through them again.

What makes \\ special compared to the other ones?
It's simply the way you would write out one backslash (\) character. Think about why you would need this.

When I write // or /n it doesn't work.
That's because you are using a forward-slash / and not a backslash \. They are different characters that do very different things.

When I use a %r format none of the escape sequences work.
That's because %r is printing out the raw representation of what you typed, which is going to include the original escape sequences. Use %s instead. Always remember this: %r is for debugging; %s is for displaying.

I don't get Study Drills #3. What do you mean by "combine" escapes and formats?
One of the things I try to get you to understand is that each of these exercises can be combined to solve problems. Take what you know about format sequences and write some new code that uses those *and* the escapes from this exercise.

What's better, ''' or """?
It's entirely based on style. Go with the ''' (triple-single-quote) style for now, but be ready to use either, depending on what feels best or what everyone else is doing.

Asking Questions

Now it is time to pick up the pace. I have got you doing a lot of printing so that you get used to typing simple things, but those simple things are fairly boring. What we want to do now is get data into your programs. This is a little tricky because you have to learn to do two things that may not make sense right away, but trust me and do it anyway. It will make sense in a few exercises.

Most of what software does is the following:

1. Take some kind of input from a person.

2. Change it.

3. Print out something to show how it changed.

So far you have only been printing, but you haven't been able to get any input from a person or change it. You may not even know what "input" means, so rather than talk about it, let's have you do some and see if you get it. In the next exercise, we'll do more to explain it.

ex11.py

```
1    print "How old are you?",
2    age = raw_input()
3    print "How tall are you?",
4    height = raw_input()
5    print "How much do you weigh?",
6    weight = raw_input()
7
8    print "So, you're %r old, %r tall and %r heavy." % (
9        age, height, weight)
```

NOTE: Notice that we put a , (comma) at the end of each print line. This is so that print doesn't end the line with a new line character and go to the next line.

What You Should See

```
$ python ex11.py
How old are you? 38
How tall are you? 6'2"
How much do you weigh? 180lbs
So, you're '38' old, '6\'2"' tall and '180lbs' heavy.
```

Study Drills

1.   Go online and find out what Python's `raw_input` does.

2.   Can you find other ways to use it? Try some of the samples you find.

3.   Write another "form" like this to ask some other questions.

4.   Related to escape sequences, try to find out why the last line has `'6\'2"'` with that `\'` sequence. See how the single-quote needs to be escaped because otherwise it would end the string?

Common Student Questions

How do I get a number from someone so I can do math?
That's a little advanced, but try x = int(raw_input()), which gets the number as a string from raw_input() then converts it to an integer using int().

I put my height into raw input like raw_input("6'2") but it doesn't work.
You don't put your height in there; you type it directly into your Terminal. First thing is, go back and make the code exactly like mine. Next, run the script, and when it pauses, type your height in at your keyboard. That's all there is to it.

Why do you have a new line on line 8 instead of putting it on one line?
That's so that the line is less than 80 characters long, which is a style that Python programmers like. You could put it on one line if you like.

What's the difference between input() and raw_input()?
The input() function will try to convert things you enter as if they were Python code, but it has security problems so you should avoid it.

When my strings print out there's a u in front of them, as in u'35'.
That's how Python tells you that the string is Unicode. Use a %s format instead and you'll see it printed like normal.

Prompting People

When you typed raw_input(), you were typing the (and) characters, which are parenthesis characters. This is similar to when you used them to do a format with extra variables, as in "%s %s" % (x, y). For raw_input, you can also put in a prompt to show to a person so he knows what to type. Put a string that you want for the prompt inside the () so that it looks like this:

```
y = raw_input("Name? ")
```

This prompts the user with "Name?" and puts the result into the variable y. This is how you ask someone a question and get the answer.

This means we can completely rewrite our previous exercise using just raw_input to do all the prompting.

ex12.py

```
1    age = raw_input("How old are you? ")
2    height = raw_input("How tall are you? ")
3    weight = raw_input("How much do you weigh? ")
4
5    print "So, you're %r old, %r tall and %r heavy." % (
6        age, height, weight)
```

What You Should See

Exercise 12 Session

```
$ python ex12.py
How old are you?  38
How tall are you?  6'2"
How much do you weigh?  180lbs
So, you're '38' old, '6\'2"' tall and '180lbs' heavy.
```

Study Drills

1. In Terminal, where you normally run python to run your scripts, type pydoc raw_input. Read what it says. If you're on Windows try python -m pydoc raw_input instead.

2. Get out of pydoc by typing q to quit.

3.   Look online for what the pydoc command does.

4.   Use pydoc to also read about open, `file`, `os`, and `sys`. It's alright if you do not under-
     stand those; just read through and take notes about interesting things.

Common Student Questions

How come I get SyntaxError: `invalid syntax` whenever I run pydoc?
You aren't running pydoc from the command line; you're probably running it from inside python.
Exit out of python first.

Why does my pydoc not pause like yours does?
Sometimes if the help document is short enough to fit on one screen, then pydoc will just print it.

When I run pydoc I get `more is not recognized as an internal`.
Some versions of Windows do not have that command, which means pydoc is broken for you.
You can skip this Study Drill and just search online for Python documentation when you need it.

Why would I use %r over %s?
Remember, %r is for debugging and is "raw representation" while %s is for display. I will not
answer this question again, so you *must* memorize this fact. This is the #1 thing people ask repeatedly, and asking the same question over and over means you aren't taking the time to memorize
what you should. Stop now, and finally memorize this fact.

Why can't I do print `"How old are you?"` , `raw_input()`?
You'd think that'd work, but Python doesn't recognize that as valid. The only answer I can really
give is, you just can't.

Parameters, Unpacking, Variables

In this exercise, we will cover one more input method you can use to pass variables to a script (script being another name for your .py files). You know how you type python ex13.py to run the ex13.py file? Well the ex13.py part of the command is called an "argument." What we'll do now is write a script that also accepts arguments.

Type this program and I'll explain it in detail:

ex13.py

```
1    from sys import argv
2
3    script, first, second, third = argv
4
5    print "The script is called:", script
6    print "Your first variable is:", first
7    print "Your second variable is:", second
8    print "Your third variable is:", third
```

On line 1 we have what's called an "import." This is how you add features to your script from the Python feature set. Rather than give you all the features at once, Python asks you to say what you plan to use. This keeps your programs small, but it also acts as documentation for other programmers who read your code later.

The argv is the "argument variable," a very standard name in programming that you will find used in many other languages. This variable *holds* the arguments you pass to your Python script when you run it. In the exercises you will get to play with this more and see what happens.

Line 3 "unpacks" argv so that, rather than holding all the arguments, it gets assigned to four variables you can work with: script, first, second, and third. This may look strange, but "unpack" is probably the best word to describe what it does. It just says, "Take whatever is in argv, unpack it, and assign it to all these variables on the left in order."

After that, we just print them out like normal.

Hold Up! Features Have Another Name

I call them "features" here (these little things you import to make your Python program do more) but nobody else calls them features. I just used that name because I needed to trick you into learning what they are without jargon. Before you can continue, you need to learn their real name: *modules*.

From now on we will be calling these "features" that we import *modules*. I'll say things like, "You want to import the sys module." They are also called "libraries" by other programmers, but let's just stick with modules.

What You Should See

Run the program like this (and you *must* pass *three* command line arguments):

Exercise 13 Session

```
$ python ex13.py first 2nd 3rd
The script is called: ex13.py
Your first variable is: first
Your second variable is: 2nd
Your third variable is: 3rd
```

This is what you should see when you do a few different runs with different arguments:

Exercise 13 Session

```
$ python ex13.py stuff things that
The script is called: ex13.py
Your first variable is: stuff
Your second variable is: things
Your third variable is: that
$
$ python ex13.py apple orange grapefruit
The script is called: ex13.py
Your first variable is: apple
Your second variable is: orange
Your third variable is: grapefruit
```

You can actually replace first, second, and third with any three things you want.

If you do not run it correctly, then you will get an error like this:

Exercise 13 Session

```
$ python ex13.py first 2nd
Traceback (most recent call last):
  File "ex13.py", line 3, in <module>
    script, first, second, third = argv
ValueError: need more than 3 values to unpack
```

This happens when you do not put enough arguments on the command when you run it (in this case just first 2nd). Notice when I run it I give it first 2nd, which caused it to give an error about "need more than 3 values to unpack," telling you that you didn't give it enough parameters.

Study Drills

1. Try giving fewer than three arguments to your script. See that error you get? See if you can explain it.

2. Write a script that has fewer arguments and one that has more. Make sure you give the unpacked variables good names.

3. Combine raw_input with argv to make a script that gets more input from a user.

4. Remember that modules give you features. Modules. Modules. Remember this because we'll need it later.

Common Student Questions

When I run it I get ValueError: need more than 1 value to unpack.
Remember that an important skill is paying attention to details. If you look at the What You Should See (WYSS) section, you see that I run the script with parameters on the command line. You should replicate how I ran it exactly.

What's the difference between argv and raw_input()?
The difference has to do with where the user is required to give input. If they give your script inputs on the command line, then you use argv. If you want them to input using the keyboard while the script is running, then use raw_input().

Are the command line arguments strings?
Yes, they come in as strings, even if you typed numbers on the command line. Use int() to convert them just like with raw_input().

How do you use the command line?
You should have learned to use it real quick by now, but if you need to learn it at this stage, then read the Command Line Crash Course appendix.

I can't combine argv with raw_input().
Don't over think it. Just slap two lines at the end of this script that uses raw_input() to get something and then print it. From that, start playing with more ways to use both in the same script.

Why can't I do this raw_input('? ') = x?
Because that's backward. Do it the way I do it and it'll work.

Prompting and Passing

Let's do one exercise that uses argv and raw_input together to ask the user something specific. You will need this for the next exercise, where we learn to read and write files. In this exercise, we'll use raw_input slightly differently by having it just print a simple > prompt. This is similar to a game like Zork or Adventure.

ex14.py

```
1    from sys import argv
2
3    script, user_name = argv
4    prompt = '> '
5
6    print "Hi %s, I'm the %s script." % (user_name, script)
7    print "I'd like to ask you a few questions."
8    print "Do you like me %s?" % user_name
9    likes = raw_input(prompt)
10
11   print "Where do you live %s?" % user_name
12   lives = raw_input(prompt)
13
14   print "What kind of computer do you have?"
15   computer = raw_input(prompt)
16
17   print """
18   Alright, so you said %r about liking me.
19   You live in %r.  Not sure where that is.
20   And you have a %r computer.  Nice.
21   """ % (likes, lives, computer)
```

Notice though that we make a variable prompt that is set to the prompt we want, and we give that to raw_input instead of typing it over and over. Now if we want to make the prompt something else, we just change it in this one spot and rerun the script.

Very handy.

What You Should See

When you run this, remember that you have to give the script your name for the argv arguments.

Exercise 14 Session

```
$ python ex14.py zed
Hi zed, I'm the ex14.py script.
```

```
I'd like to ask you a few questions.
Do you like me zed?
>  Yes
Where do you live zed?
>  San Francisco
What kind of computer do you have?
>  Tandy 1000

Alright, so you said 'Yes' about liking me.
You live in 'San Francisco'.  Not sure where that is.
And you have a 'Tandy 1000' computer.  Nice.
```

Study Drills

1. Find out what Zork and Adventure were. Try to find a copy and play it.

2. Change the prompt variable to something else entirely.

3. Add another argument and use it in your script.

4. Make sure you understand how I combined a """ style multiline string with the % format activator as the last print.

Common Student Questions

I get SyntaxError: `invalid syntax` when I run this script.
Again, you have to run it right on the command line, not inside Python. If you type python and then try to type `python ex14.py Zed`, it will fail because you are running *Python inside Python*. Close your window and then just type `python ex14.py Zed`.

I don't understand what you mean by changing the prompt?
See the variable `prompt = '> '`. Change that to have a different value. You know this; it's just a string and you've done 13 exercises making them, so take the time to figure it out.

I get the error `ValueError: need more than 1 value to unpack`.
Remember when I said you need to look at the WYSS section and replicate what I did? You need to do the same thing here and focus on how I type the command in and why I have a command line argument.

Can I use double-quotes for the prompt variable?
You totally can. Go ahead and try that.

You have a Tandy computer?
I did when I was little.

I get `NameError: name 'prompt' is not defined` **when I run it.**
You either spelled the name of the `prompt` variable wrong or forgot that line. Go back and compare each line of code to mine, and start at the bottom of the script and work your way to the top.

How can I run this from IDLE?
Don't use IDLE.

Reading Files

Everything you've learned about raw_input and argv is so you can start reading files. You may have to play with this exercise the most to understand what's going on, so do it carefully and remember your checks. Working with files is an easy way to *erase your work* if you are not careful.

This exercise involves writing two files. One is your usual ex15.py file that you will run, but the *other* is named ex15_sample.txt. This second file isn't a script but a plain text file we'll be reading in our script. Here are the contents of that file:

```
This is stuff I typed into a file.
It is really cool stuff.
Lots and lots of fun to have in here.
```

What we want to do is "open" that file in our script and print it out. However, we do not want to just "hard code" the name ex15_sample.txt into our script. "Hard coding" means putting some bit of information that should come from the user as a string right in our program. That's bad because we want it to load other files later. The solution is to use argv and raw_input to ask the user what file the user wants instead of "hard coding" the file's name.

ex15.py

```
1    from sys import argv
2
3    script, filename = argv
4
5    txt = open(filename)
6
7    print "Here's your file %r:" % filename
8    print txt.read()
9
10   print "Type the filename again:"
11   file_again = raw_input("> ")
12
13   txt_again = open(file_again)
14
15   print txt_again.read()
```

A few fancy things are going on in this file, so let's break it down real quick:

Lines 1–3 should be a familiar use of argv to get a filename. Next we have line 5 where we use a new command open. Right now, run pydoc open and read the instructions. Notice how like your own scripts and raw_input, it takes a parameter and returns a value you can set to your own variable. You just opened a file.

Line 7 we print a little line, but on line 8 we have something very new and exciting. We call a function on txt. What you got back from open is a file, and it's also got commands you can give it. You give a file a command by using the . (dot or period), the name of the command, and parameters. Just like with open and raw_input. The difference is that when you say txt.read() you are saying, "Hey txt! Do your read command with no parameters!"

The remainder of the file is more of the same, but we'll leave the analysis to you in the Study Drills.

What You Should See

I made a file called "ex15_sample.txt" and ran my script.

```
$ python ex15.py ex15_sample.txt
Here's your file 'ex15_sample.txt':
This is stuff I typed into a file.
It is really cool stuff.
Lots and lots of fun to have in here.


Type the filename again:
>  ex15_sample.txt
This is stuff I typed into a file.
It is really cool stuff.
Lots and lots of fun to have in here.
```

Study Drills

This is a big jump, so be sure you do this Study Drill as best you can before moving on.

1. Above each line, write out in English what that line does.

2. If you are not sure, ask someone for help or search online. Many times searching for "python THING" will find answers for what that THING does in Python. Try searching for "python open."

3. I used the name "commands" here, but they are also called "functions" and "methods." Search around online to see what other people do to define these. Do not worry if they confuse you. It's normal for programmers to confuse you with vast extensive knowledge.

4. Get rid of the part from lines 10–15 where you use raw_input and try the script then.

5. Use only raw_input and try the script that way. Think of why one way of getting the filename would be better than another.

6. Run pydoc `file` and scroll down until you see the `read()` command (method/function). See all the other ones you can use? Skip the ones that have __ (two underscores) in front because those are junk. Try some of the other commands.

7. Start python again and use open from the prompt. Notice how you can open files and run read on them right there?

8. Have your script also do a `close()` on the `txt` and `txt_again` variables. It's important to close files when you are done with them.

Common Student Questions

Does `txt = open(filename)` return the contents of the file?
No, it doesn't. It actually makes something called a "file object." You can think of it like an old tape drive that you saw on mainframe computers in the 1950s or even like a DVD player from today. You can move around inside them, and then "read" them, but the file is not the contents.

I can't type code into my Terminal/PowerShell like you say in Study Drill #7.
First thing, from the command line just type python and hit Enter. Now you are in python as we've done a few other times. Once you have that you can just type in code and Python will run it in little pieces. Play with that. To get out of it type quit() and hit Enter.

What does `from sys import argv` mean?
For now, just understand that sys is a package, and this phrase just says to get the argv feature from that package. You'll learn more about these later.

I put the name of the file in as `script, ex15_sample.txt = argv` but it doesn't work.
No, that's not how you do it. Make the code exactly like mine, then run it from the command line the exact same way I do. You don't put the names of files in; you let Python put the name in.

Why is there no error when we open the file twice?
Python will not restrict you from opening a file more than once, and in fact sometimes this is necessary.

Reading and Writing Files

If you did the Study Drills from the last exercise, you should have seen all sorts of commands (methods/functions) you can give to files. Here's the list of commands I want you to remember:

- close—Closes the file. Like File->Save.. in your editor.

- read—Reads the contents of the file. You can assign the result to a variable.

- readline—Reads just one line of a text file.

- truncate—Empties the file. Watch out if you care about the file.

- write(stuff)—Writes stuff to the file.

For now, these are the important commands you need to know. Some of them take parameters, but we do not really care about that. You only need to remember that write takes a parameter of a string you want to write to the file.

Let's use some of this to make a simple little text editor:

ex16.py

```
1    from sys import argv
2
3    script, filename = argv
4
5    print "We're going to erase %r." % filename
6    print "If you don't want that, hit CTRL-C (^C)."
7    print "If you do want that, hit RETURN."
8
9    raw_input("?")
10
11   print "Opening the file..."
12   target = open(filename, 'w')
13
14   print "Truncating the file.  Goodbye!"
15   target.truncate()
16
17   print "Now I'm going to ask you for three lines."
18
19   line1 = raw_input("line 1: ")
20   line2 = raw_input("line 2: ")
21   line3 = raw_input("line 3: ")
22
23   print "I'm going to write these to the file."
24
25   target.write(line1)
26   target.write("\n")
```

```
27    target.write(line2)
28    target.write("\n")
29    target.write(line3)
30    target.write("\n")
31
32    print "And finally, we close it."
33    target.close()
```

That's a large file—probably the largest you have typed in. So go slow, do your checks, and make it run. One trick is to get bits of it running at a time. Get lines 1–8 running, then five more, then a few more, and so on, until it's all done and running.

What You Should See

There are actually two things you will see. First the output of your new script:

Exercise 16 Session

```
$ python ex16.py test.txt
We're going to erase 'test.txt'.
If you don't want that, hit CTRL-C (^C).
If you do want that, hit RETURN.
?
Opening the file...
Truncating the file.  Goodbye!
Now I'm going to ask you for three lines.
line 1:  Mary had a little lamb
line 2:  It's fleece was white as snow
line 3:  It was also tasty
I'm going to write these to the file.
And finally, we close it.
```

Now, open up the file you made (in my case test.txt) in your editor and check it out. Neat, right?

Study Drills

1. If you feel you do not understand this, go back through and use the comment trick to get it squared away in your mind. One simple English comment above each line will help you understand or at least let you know what you need to research more.

2. Write a script similar to the last exercise that uses read and argv to read the file you just created.

3. There's too much repetition in this file. Use strings, formats, and escapes to print out line1, line2, and line3 with just one target.write() command instead of six.

4. Find out why we had to pass a `'w'` as an extra parameter to open. Hint: open tries to be safe by making you explicitly say you want to write a file.

5. If you open the file with `'w'` mode, then do you really need the `target.truncate()`? Go read the docs for Python's open function and see if that's true.

Common Student Questions

Is the `truncate()` necessary with the `'w'` parameter?
See Study Drills #5.

What does `'w'` mean?
It's really just a string with a character in it for the kind of mode for the file. If you use `'w'`, then you're saying "open this file in 'write' mode"—hence the `'w'` character. There's also `'r'` for "read," `'a'` for append, and modifiers on these.

What are the modifiers to the file modes we can use?
The most important one to know for now is the + modifier, so you can do `'w+'`, `'r+'`, and `'a+'`. This will open the file in both read and write mode and, depending on the character used, position the file in different ways.

Does just doing open(`filename`) open it in `'r'` (read) mode?
Yes, that's the default for the `open()` function.

More Files

Now let's do a few more things with files. We're going to actually write a Python script to copy one file to another. It'll be very short but will give you some ideas about other things you can do with files.

ex17.py

```
1    from sys import argv
2    from os.path import exists
3
4    script, from_file, to_file = argv
5
6    print "Copying from %s to %s" % (from_file, to_file)
7
8    # we could do these two on one line too, how?
9    in_file = open(from_file)
10   indata = in_file.read()
11
12   print "The input file is %d bytes long" % len(indata)
13
14   print "Does the output file exist? %r" % exists(to_file)
15   print "Ready, hit RETURN to continue, CTRL-C to abort."
16   raw_input()
17
18   out_file = open(to_file, 'w')
19   out_file.write(indata)
20
21   print "Alright, all done."
22
23   out_file.close()
24   in_file.close()
```

You should immediately notice that we import another handy command named exists. This returns True if a file exists, based on its name in a string as an argument. It returns False if not. We'll be using this function in the second half of this book to do lots of things, but right now you should see how you can import it.

Using import is a way to get tons of free code other better (well, usually) programmers have written so you do not have to write it.

What You Should See

Just like your other scripts, run this one with two arguments: the file to copy from and the file to copy it to. I'm going to use a simple test file named test.txt again:

```
$ cat test.txt
This is a test file.
$
$ python ex17.py test.txt new_file.txt
Copying from test.txt to new_file.txt
The input file is 21 bytes long
Does the output file exist? False
Ready, hit RETURN to continue, CTRL-C to abort.

Alright, all done.
```

It should work with any file. Try a bunch more and see what happens. Just be careful you do not blast an important file.

WARNING! Did you see that trick I did with cat to show the file? You can learn how to do that in the appendix.

Study Drills

1. Go read up on Python's import statement, and start python to try it out. Try importing some things and see if you can get it right. It's alright if you do not.

2. This script is *really* annoying. There's no need to ask you before doing the copy, and it prints too much out to the screen. Try to make it more friendly to use by removing features.

3. See how short you can make the script. I could make this one line long.

4. Notice at the end of the WYSS I used something called cat? It's an old command that "concatenates" files together, but mostly it's just an easy way to print a file to the screen. Type man cat to read about it.

5. Windows people, find the alternative to cat that Linux/OSX people have. Do not worry about man since there is nothing like that.

6. Find out why you had to do output.close() in the code.

Common Student Questions

Why is the 'w' in quotes?
That's a string. You've been using them for a while now, so make sure you know what a string is.

No way you can make this one line!
That ; depends ; on ; how ; you ; define ; one ; line ; of ; code.

What does the `len()` function do?
It gets the length of the string that you pass to it and then returns that as a number. Play with it.

When I try to make this script shorter, I get an error when I close the files at the end.
You probably did something like this, `indata = open(from_file).read()`, which means you don't need to then do `in_file.close()` when you reach the end of the script. It should already be closed by Python once that one line runs.

Is it normal to feel like this exercise was really hard?
Yes, it is totally normal. Programming may not "click" for you until maybe even Exercise 36, or it might not until you finish the book and then make something with Python. Everyone is different, so just keep going and keep reviewing exercises that you had trouble with until it clicks. Be patient.

I get a `Syntax:EOL while scanning string literal` error.
You forgot to end a string properly with a quote. Go look at that line again.

Names, Variables, Code, Functions

Big title, right? I am about to introduce you to *the function*! Dum dum dah! Every programmer will go on and on about functions and all the different ideas about how they work and what they do, but I will give you the simplest explanation you can use right now.

Functions do three things:

1. They name pieces of code the way variables name strings and numbers.

2. They take arguments the way your scripts take argv.

3. Using #1 and #2, they let you make your own "mini-scripts" or "tiny commands."

You can create a function by using the word def in Python. I'm going to have you make four different functions that work like your scripts, and I'll then show you how each one is related.

ex18.py

```
1   # this one is like your scripts with argv
2   def print_two(*args):
3       arg1, arg2 = args
4       print "arg1: %r, arg2: %r" % (arg1, arg2)
5
6   # ok, that *args is actually pointless, we can just do this
7   def print_two_again(arg1, arg2):
8       print "arg1: %r, arg2: %r" % (arg1, arg2)
9
10  # this just takes one argument
11  def print_one(arg1):
12      print "arg1: %r" % arg1
13
14  # this one takes no arguments
15  def print_none():
16      print "I got nothin'."
17
18
19  print_two("Zed","Shaw")
20  print_two_again("Zed","Shaw")
21  print_one("First!")
22  print_none()
```

Let's break down the first function, print_two, which is the most similar to what you already know from making scripts:

1. First we tell Python we want to make a function using def for "define."

2. On the same line as def, we then give the function a name. In this case, we just called it print_two, but it could be peanuts too. It doesn't matter, except that your function should have a short name that says what it does.

3. Then we tell it we want *args (asterisk args), which is a lot like your argv parameter but for functions. This *has* to go inside () parentheses to work.

4. Then we end this line with a : colon and start indenting.

5. After the colon all the lines that are indented four spaces will become attached to this name, print_two. Our first indented line is one that unpacks the arguments the same as with your scripts.

6. To demonstrate how it works, we print these arguments out, just like we would in a script.

Now, the problem with print_two is that it's not the easiest way to make a function. In Python we can skip the whole unpacking args and just use the names we want right inside (). That's what print_two_again does.

After that, you have an example of how you make a function that takes one argument in print_one.

Finally you have a function that has no arguments in print_none.

WARNING! This is very important. Do *not* get discouraged right now if this doesn't quite make sense. We're going to do a few exercises linking functions to your scripts and show you how to make more. For now just keep thinking "mini-script" when I say "function," and keep playing with them.

What You Should See

If you run the above script, you should see the following:

Exercise 18 Session

```
$ python ex18.py
arg1: 'Zed', arg2: 'Shaw'
arg1: 'Zed', arg2: 'Shaw'
arg1: 'First!'
I got nothin'.
```

Right away you can see how a function works. Notice that you used your functions the way you use things like exists, open, and other "commands." In fact, I've been tricking you because in Python those "commands" are just functions. This means you can make your own commands and use them in your scripts too.

Study Drills

Write out a `function checklist` for later exercises. Write these on an index card and keep it by you while you complete the rest of these exercises or until you feel you do not need it:

1. Did you start your function definition with `def`?

2. Does your function name have only characters and _ (underscore) characters?

3. Did you put an open parenthesis `(` right after the function name?

4. Did you put your arguments after the parenthesis `(` separated by commas?

5. Did you make each argument unique (meaning no duplicated names)?

6. Did you put a close parenthesis and a colon `)`: after the arguments?

7. Did you indent all lines of code you want in the function four spaces? No more, no less.

8. Did you "end" your function by going back to writing with no indent (dedenting we call it)?

And when you run ("use" or "call") a function, check these things:

1. Did you call/use/run this function by typing its name?

2. Did you put the `(` character after the name to run it?

3. Did you put the values you want into the parenthesis separated by commas?

4. Did you end the function call with a `)` character?

Use these two checklists on the remaining lessons until you do not need them anymore. Finally, repeat this a few times: "To 'run,' 'call,' or 'use' a function all mean the same thing."

Common Student Questions

What's allowed for a function name?
Just like variable names, anything that doesn't start with a number and is letters, numbers, and underscores will work.

What does the * in *args do?
That tells Python to take all the arguments to the function and then put them in args as a list. It's like `argv` that you've been using, but for functions. It's not normally used too often unless specifically needed.

This feels really boring and monotonous.
That's good. It means you're starting to get better at typing in the code and understanding what it does. To make it less boring, take everything I tell you to type in, and then break it on purpose.

Functions and Variables

Functions may have been a mind-blowing amount of information, but do not worry. Just keep doing these exercises and going through your checklist from the last exercise and you will eventually get it.

There is one tiny point though that you might not have realized, which we'll reinforce right now. The variables in your function are not connected to the variables in your script. Here's an exercise to get you thinking about this:

ex19.py

```
1    def cheese_and_crackers(cheese_count, boxes_of_crackers):
2        print "You have %d cheeses!" % cheese_count
3        print "You have %d boxes of crackers!" % boxes_of_crackers
4        print "Man that's enough for a party!"
5        print "Get a blanket.\n"
6
7
8    print "We can just give the function numbers directly:"
9    cheese_and_crackers(20, 30)
10
11
12   print "OR, we can use variables from our script:"
13   amount_of_cheese = 10
14   amount_of_crackers = 50
15
16   cheese_and_crackers(amount_of_cheese, amount_of_crackers)
17
18
19   print "We can even do math inside too:"
20   cheese_and_crackers(10 + 20, 5 + 6)
21
22
23   print "And we can combine the two, variables and math:"
24   cheese_and_crackers(amount_of_cheese + 100, amount_of_crackers + 1000)
```

This shows all the different ways we're able to give our function cheese_and_crackers the values it needs to print them. We can give it straight numbers. We can give it variables. We can give it math. We can even combine math and variables.

In a way, the arguments to a function are kind of like our = character when we make a variable. In fact, if you can use = to name something, you can usually pass it to a function as an argument.

What You Should See

You should study the output of this script and compare it with what you think you should get for each of the examples in the script.

```
$ python ex19.py
We can just give the function numbers directly:
You have 20 cheeses!
You have 30 boxes of crackers!
Man that's enough for a party!
Get a blanket.

OR, we can use variables from our script:
You have 10 cheeses!
You have 50 boxes of crackers!
Man that's enough for a party!
Get a blanket.

We can even do math inside too:
You have 30 cheeses!
You have 11 boxes of crackers!
Man that's enough for a party!
Get a blanket.

And we can combine the two, variables and math:
You have 110 cheeses!
You have 1050 boxes of crackers!
Man that's enough for a party!
Get a blanket.
```

Study Drills

1. Go back through the script and type a comment above each line, explaining in English what it does.

2. Start at the bottom and read each line backward, saying all the important characters.

3. Write at least one more function of your own design, and run it 10 different ways.

Common Student Questions

How can there possibly be 10 different ways to run a function?
Believe it or not, there's a theoretically infinite number of ways to call any function. In this case, do it like I've got with lines 8–12 and be creative.

Is there a way to analyze what this function is doing so I can understand it better?
There's many different ways, but try putting an English comment above each line describing what the line does. Another trick is to read the code out loud. Yet another is to print the code out and draw on the paper with pictures and comments showing what's going on.

What if I want to ask the user for the numbers of cheese and crackers?
Remember, you just need to use `int()` to convert what you get from `raw_input()`.

Does making the variables on lines 13 and 14 change the variables in the function?
Nope, those variables are separate and live outside the function. They are then passed to the function and temporary versions are made just for the function's run. When the function exits, these temporary variables go away and everything keeps working. Keep going in the book and this should become clearer.

Is it bad to have global variables (like on lines 13 and 14) with the same name as function variables?
Yes, since then you're not quite sure which one you're talking about. But sometimes necessity means you have to use the same name, or you might do it on accident. Just avoid it whenever you can.

Are lines 12–19 overwriting the function `cheese_and_crackers`**?**
No, not at all. It's calling them, which is basically a temporary jump to the first line of the function, then a jump back after the last line of the function has ended. It's not replacing the function with anything.

Is there a limit to the number of arguments a function can have?
It depends on the version of Python and the computer you're on, but it is fairly large. The practical limit, though, is about five arguments before the function becomes annoying to use.

Can you call a function within a function?
Yes, you'll make a game that does this later in the book.

Functions and Files

Remember your checklist for functions, then do this exercise paying close attention to how functions and files can work together to make useful stuff.

ex20.py

```
1    from sys import argv
2
3    script, input_file = argv
4
5    def print_all(f):
6        print f.read()
7
8    def rewind(f):
9        f.seek(0)
10
11   def print_a_line(line_count, f):
12       print line_count, f.readline()
13
14   current_file = open(input_file)
15
16   print "First let's print the whole file:\n"
17
18   print_all(current_file)
19
20   print "Now let's rewind, kind of like a tape."
21
22   rewind(current_file)
23
24   print "Let's print three lines:"
25
26   current_line = 1
27   print_a_line(current_line, current_file)
28
29   current_line = current_line + 1
30   print_a_line(current_line, current_file)
31
32   current_line = current_line + 1
33   print_a_line(current_line, current_file)
```

Pay close attention to how we pass in the current line number each time we run print_a_line.

What You Should See

```
$ python ex20.py test.txt
First let's print the whole file:

This is line 1
This is line 2
This is line 3

Now let's rewind, kind of like a tape.
Let's print three lines:
1 This is line 1

2 This is line 2

3 This is line 3
```

Study Drills

1. Go through and write English comments for each line to understand what's going on.

2. Each time print_a_line is run, you are passing in a variable current_line. Write out what current_line is equal to on each function call, and trace how it becomes line_count in print_a_line.

3. Find each place a function is used, and go check its def to make sure that you are giving it the right arguments.

4. Research online what the seek function for file does. Try pydoc file and see if you can figure it out from there.

5. Research the shorthand notation += and rewrite the script to use that.

Common Student Questions

What is f in the print_all and other functions?
The f is a variable just like you had in other functions in Exercise 18, except this time it's a file. A file in Python is kind of like an old tape drive on a mainframe, or maybe a DVD player. It has a "read head," and you can "seek" this read head around the file to positions, then work with it there. Each time you do f.seek(0), you're moving to the start of the file. Each time you do

`f.readline()`, you're reading a line from the file and moving the read head to right after the \n that ends that file. This will be explained more as you go on.

Why are there empty lines between the lines in the file?
The `readline()` function returns the \n that's in the file at the end of that line. This means that print's \n is being added to the one already returned by `readline()`. To change this behavior simply add a , (comma) at the end of print so that it doesn't print its own \n.

Why does seek(0) not set the `current_line` to 0?
First, the `seek()` function is dealing in *bytes*, not lines. So that's going to the 0 byte (first byte) in the file. Second, `current_line` is just a variable and has no real connection to the file at all. We are manually incrementing it.

What is +=?
You know how in English I can rewrite "it is" to be "it's"? Or I can rewrite "you are" to "you're"? That's called a contraction, and this is kind of like a contraction for the two operations = and +. That means x = x + y is the same as x += y.

How does readline() know where each line is?
Inside `readline()` is code that scans each byte of the file until it finds a \n character, then stops reading the file to return what it found so far. The file f is responsible for maintaining the current position in the file after each `readline()` call, so that it will keep reading each line.

Functions Can Return Something

You have been using the = character to name variables and set them to numbers or strings. We're now going to blow your mind again by showing you how to use = and a new Python word return to set variables to be a *value from a function*. There will be one thing to pay close attention to, but first type this in:

```
1    def add(a, b):
2        print "ADDING %d + %d" % (a, b)
3        return a + b
4
5    def subtract(a, b):
6        print "SUBTRACTING %d - %d" % (a, b)
7        return a - b
8
9    def multiply(a, b):
10       print "MULTIPLYING %d * %d" % (a, b)
11       return a * b
12
13   def divide(a, b):
14       print "DIVIDING %d / %d" % (a, b)
15       return a / b
16
17
18   print "Let's do some math with just functions!"
19
20   age = add(30, 5)
21   height = subtract(78, 4)
22   weight = multiply(90, 2)
23   iq = divide(100, 2)
24
25   print "Age: %d, Height: %d, Weight: %d, IQ: %d" % (age, height, weight, iq)
26
27
28   # A puzzle for the extra credit, type it in anyway.
29   print "Here is a puzzle."
30
31   what = add(age, subtract(height, multiply(weight, divide(iq, 2))))
32
33   print "That becomes: ", what, "Can you do it by hand?"
```

We are now doing our own math functions for add, subtract, multiply, and divide. The important thing to notice is the last line where we say return a + b (in add). What this does is the following:

1. Our function is called with two arguments: a and b.

2. We print out what our function is doing, in this case ADDING.

3. Then we tell Python to do something kind of backward: we return the addition of a + b. You might say this as, "I add a and b, then return them."

4. Python adds the two numbers. Then when the function ends, any line that runs it will be able to assign this a + b result to a variable.

As with many other things in this book, you should take this real slow, break it down, and try to trace what's going on. To help there's extra credit to get you to solve a puzzle and learn something cool.

What You Should See

```
$ python ex21.py
Let's do some math with just functions!
ADDING 30 + 5
SUBTRACTING 78 - 4
MULTIPLYING 90 * 2
DIVIDING 100 / 2
Age: 35, Height: 74, Weight: 180, IQ: 50
Here is a puzzle.
DIVIDING 50 / 2
MULTIPLYING 180 * 25
SUBTRACTING 74 - 4500
ADDING 35 + -4426
That becomes:  -4391 Can you do it by hand?
```

Study Drills

1. If you aren't really sure what `return` does, try writing a few of your own functions and have them return some values. You can return anything that you can put to the right of an =.

2. At the end of the script is a puzzle. I'm taking the return value of one function and *using* it as the argument of another function. I'm doing this in a chain so that I'm kind of creating a formula using the functions. It looks really weird, but if you run the script, you can see the results. What you should do is try to figure out the normal formula that would recreate this same set of operations.

3. Once you have the formula worked out for the puzzle, get in there and see what happens when you modify the parts of the functions. Try to change it on purpose to make another value.

4. Finally, do the inverse. Write out a simple formula and use the functions in the same way to calculate it.

This exercise might really whack your brain out, but take it slow and easy and treat it like a little game. Figuring out puzzles like this is what makes programming fun, so I'll be giving you more little problems like this as we go.

Common Student Questions

Why does Python print the formula or the functions "backward"?
It's not really backward; it's "inside out." When you start breaking down the function into separate formulas and function calls, you'll see how it works. Try to understand what I mean by "inside out" rather than "backward."

How can I use `raw_input()` to enter my own values?
Remember `int(raw_input())`? The problem with that is then you can't enter floating point, so also try using `float(raw_input())` instead.

What do you mean by "write out a formula"?
Try 24 + 34 / 100 - 1023 as a start. Convert that to use the functions. Now come up with your own similar math equation and use variables so it's more like a formula.

What Do You Know So Far?

There won't be any code in this exercise or the next one, so there's no WYSS or Study Drills either. In fact, this exercise is like one giant Study Drills section. I'm going to have you do a form of review of what you have learned so far.

First, go back through every exercise you have done so far and write down every word and symbol (another name for "character") that you have used. Make sure your list of symbols is complete.

Next to each word or symbol, write its name and what it does. If you can't find a name for a symbol in this book, then look for it online. If you do not know what a word or symbol does, then go read about it again and try using it in some code.

You may run into a few things you just can't find out or know, so just keep those on the list and be ready to look them up when you find them.

Once you have your list, spend a few days rewriting the list and double-checking that it's correct. This may get boring, but push through and really nail it down.

Once you have memorized the list and what they do, then you should step it up by writing out tables of symbols, their names, and what they do *from memory*. When you hit some you can't recall from memory, go back and memorize them again.

WARNING! The most important thing when doing this exercise is: "There is no failure, only trying."

What You Are Learning

It's important when you are doing a boring, mindless memorization exercise like this to know why. It helps you focus on a goal and know the purpose of all your efforts.

In this exercise, you are learning the names of symbols so that you can read source code more easily. It's similar to learning the alphabet and basic words of English, except this Python alphabet has extra symbols you might not know.

Just take it slow and do not hurt your brain. Hopefully by now these symbols are natural for you, so this isn't a big effort. It's best to take 15 minutes at a time with your list and then take a break. Giving your brain a rest will help you learn faster with less frustration.

Read Some Code

You should have spent the last week getting your list of symbols straight and locked in your mind. Now you get to apply this to another week of reading code on the internet. This exercise will be daunting at first. I'm going to throw you in the deep end for a few days and have you just try your best to read and understand some source code from real projects. The goal isn't to get you to understand code, but to teach you the following three skills:

1. Finding Python source code for things you need.

2. Reading through the code and looking for files.

3. Trying to understand code you find.

At your level, you really do not have the skills to evaluate the things you find, but you can benefit from getting exposure and seeing how things look.

When you do this exercise, think of yourself as an anthropologist, trucking through a new land with just barely enough of the local language to get around and survive. Except, of course, that you will actually get out alive because the internet isn't a jungle.

Here's what you do:

1. Go to bitbucket.org, github.com, or gitorious.org with your favorite web browser and search for "python."

2. Avoid any project that mentions "Python 3." That'll only confuse you.

3. Pick a random project and click on it.

4. Click on the Source tab and browse through the list of files and directories until you find a .py file (but not setup.py—that's useless).

5. Start at the top and read through it, taking notes on what you think it does.

6. If any symbols or strange words seem to interest you, write them down to research later.

That's it. Your job is to use what you know so far and see if you can read the code and get a grasp of what it does. Try skimming the code first, and then read it in detail. Maybe also try to take very difficult parts and read each symbol you know out loud.

Now try some of these other sites:

- launchpad.net
- sourceforge.net
- freecode.com

More Practice

You are getting to the end of this section. You should have enough Python "under your fingers" to move on to learning about how programming really works, but you should do some more practice. This exercise is longer and all about building up stamina. The next exercise will be similar. Do them, get them exactly right, and do your checks.

ex24.py

```
1    print "Let's practice everything."
2    print 'You\'d need to know \'bout escapes with \\ that do \n newlines and \t tabs.'
3
4    poem = """
5    \tThe lovely world
6    with logic so firmly planted
7    cannot discern \n the needs of love
8    nor comprehend passion from intuition
9    and requires an explanation
10   \n\t\twhere there is none.
11   """
12
13   print "--------------"
14   print poem
15   print "--------------"
16
17
18   five = 10 - 2 + 3 - 6
19   print "This should be five: %s" % five
20
21   def secret_formula(started):
22       jelly_beans = started * 500
23       jars = jelly_beans / 1000
24       crates = jars / 100
25       return jelly_beans, jars, crates
26
27
28   start_point = 10000
29   beans, jars, crates = secret_formula(start_point)
30
31   print "With a starting point of: %d" % start_point
32   print "We'd have %d beans, %d jars, and %d crates." % (beans, jars, crates)
33
34   start_point = start_point / 10
35
36   print "We can also do that this way:"
37   print "We'd have %d beans, %d jars, and %d crates." % secret_formula(start_point)
```

What You Should See

```
$ python ex24.py
Let's practice everything.
You'd need to know 'bout escapes with \ that do
  newlines and          tabs.
--------------


        The lovely world
with logic so firmly planted
cannot discern
 the needs of love
nor comprehend passion from intuition
and requires an explanation


        where there is none.


--------------
This should be five: 5
With a starting point of: 10000
We'd have 5000000 beans, 5000 jars, and 50 crates.
We can also do that this way:
We'd have 500000 beans, 500 jars, and 5 crates.
```

Study Drills

1. Make sure to do your checks: read it backward, read it out loud, and put comments above confusing parts.

2. Break the file on purpose, then run it to see what kinds of errors you get. Make sure you can fix it.

Common Student Questions

How come you call the variable `jelly_beans` but the name beans later?
That's part of how a function works. Remember that inside the function the variable is temporary, and when you return it, then it can be assigned to a variable for later. I'm just making a new variable named beans to hold the return value.

What do you mean by reading the code backward?
Start at the last line. Compare that line in your file to the same line in mine. Once it's exactly the same, move up to the next line. Do this until you get to the first line of the file.

Who wrote that poem?
I did. Not all my poems suck.

Even More Practice

We're going to do some more practice involving functions and variables to make sure you know them well. This exercise should be straightforward for you to type in, break down, and understand.

However, this exercise is a little different. You won't be running it. Instead *you* will import it into Python and run the functions yourself.

ex25.py

```
1    def break_words(stuff):
2        """This function will break up words for us."""
3        words = stuff.split(' ')
4        return words
5
6    def sort_words(words):
7        """Sorts the words."""
8        return sorted(words)
9
10   def print_first_word(words):
11       """Prints the first word after popping it off."""
12       word = words.pop(0)
13       print word
14
15   def print_last_word(words):
16       """Prints the last word after popping it off."""
17       word = words.pop(-1)
18       print word
19
20   def sort_sentence(sentence):
21       """Takes in a full sentence and returns the sorted words."""
22       words = break_words(sentence)
23       return sort_words(words)
24
25   def print_first_and_last(sentence):
26       """Prints the first and last words of the sentence."""
27       words = break_words(sentence)
28       print_first_word(words)
29       print_last_word(words)
30
31   def print_first_and_last_sorted(sentence):
32       """Sorts the words then prints the first and last one."""
33       words = sort_sentence(sentence)
34       print_first_word(words)
35       print_last_word(words)
```

First, run this like normal with `python ex25.py` to find any errors you have made. Once you have found all the errors you can and fixed them, you will then want to follow the WYSS section to complete the exercise.

What You Should See

In this exercise, we're going to interact with your `.py` file inside the python interpreter you used periodically to do calculations. You run that from the shell like this:

```
$ python
Python 2.7.1 (r271:86832, Jun 16 2011, 16:59:05)
[GCC 4.2.1 (Based on Apple Inc. build 5658) (LLVM build 2335.15.00)] on darwin
Type "help", "copyright", "credits" or "license" for more information.
>>>
```

Yours will look a little different from mine, but once you see the >>> prompt you can then type Python code in and it will run immediately.

Here's what it looks like when I do it:

Exercise 25 Python Session

```
Python 2.7.1 (r271:86832, Jun 16 2011, 16:59:05)
[GCC 4.2.1 (Based on Apple Inc. build 5658) (LLVM build 2335.15.00)] on darwin
Type "help", "copyright", "credits" or "license" for more information.
>>> import ex25
>>> sentence = "All good things come to those who wait."
>>> words = ex25.break_words(sentence)
>>> words
['All', 'good', 'things', 'come', 'to', 'those', 'who', 'wait.']
>>> sorted_words = ex25.sort_words(words)
>>> sorted_words
['All', 'come', 'good', 'things', 'those', 'to', 'wait.', 'who']
>>> ex25.print_first_word(words)
All
>>> ex25.print_last_word(words)
wait.
>>> wrods
Traceback (most recent call last):
  File "<stdin>", line 1, in <module>
NameError: name 'wrods' is not defined
>>> words
['good', 'things', 'come', 'to', 'those', 'who']
>>> ex25.print_first_word(sorted_words)
All
>>> ex25.print_last_word(sorted_words)
who
>>> sorted_words
```

```
['come', 'good', 'things', 'those', 'to', 'wait.']
>>> sorted_words = ex25.sort_sentence(sentence)
>>> sorted_words
['All', 'come', 'good', 'things', 'those', 'to', 'wait.', 'who']
>>> ex25.print_first_and_last(sentence)
All
wait.
>>> ex25.print_first_and_last_sorted(sentence)
All
who
```

Let's break this down line by line to make sure you know what's going on:

- **Line 5.** You import *your* ex25.py Python file, just like other imports you have done. Notice you do not need to put the .py at the end to import it. When you do this, you make a module that has all your functions in it to use.

- **Line 6.** You made a sentence to work with.

- **Line 7.** You use the ex25 module and call your first function ex25.break_words. The . (dot, period) symbol is how you tell Python, "Hey, inside ex25 there's a function called break_words and I want to run it."

- **Line 8.** We just type words, and Python will print out what's in that variable (line 9). It looks weird, but this is a list that you will learn about later.

- **Lines 10–11.** We do the same thing with ex25.sort_words to get a sorted sentence.

- **Lines 13–16.** We use ex25.print_first_word and ex25.print_last_word to get the first and last word printed out.

- **Line 17.** This is interesting. I made a mistake and typed the words variable as wrods so Python gave me an error on lines 18–20.

- **Lines 21–22.** We print the modified words list. Notice that since we printed the first and last one, those words are now missing.

The remaining lines are for you to figure out and analyze in the Study Drills.

Study Drills

1. Take the remaining lines of the WYSS output and figure out what they are doing. Make sure you understand how you are running your functions in the ex25 module.

2. Try doing this: help(ex25) and also help(ex25.break_words). Notice how you get help for your module and how the help is those odd """ strings you put after each func-

tion in ex25? Those special strings are called documentation comments and we'll be seeing more of them.

3.   Typing ex25. is annoying. A shortcut is to do your import like this: from ex25 import *, which is like saying, "Import everything from ex25." Programmers like saying things backward. Start a new session and see how all your functions are right there.

4.   Try breaking your file and see what it looks like in Python when you use it. You will have to quit Python with CTRL-D (CTRL-Z on Windows) to be able to reload it.

Common Student Questions

I get a None printed out for some of the functions.
You probably have a function that is missing the return at the end. Go backward through the file like I taught you and confirm that every line is right.

I get -bash: import: command not found when I type import ex25.
Pay attention to what I'm doing in the WYSS section. I'm doing this in *Python,* not in the Terminal. That means you first run Python.

I get ImportError: No module named ex25.py when I type import ex25.py.
Don't add the .py to the end. Python knows the file ends in .py, so you just type import ex25.

I get SyntaxError: invalid syntax when I run this.
That means you have something like a missing (or " or similar syntax error on that line or above it. Any time you get that error, start at the line it mentions and check that it's right, then go backward, checking each line above that.

How can the words.pop(0) be changing the words variable then?
That's a complicated question, but in this case words is a list, and because of that you can give it commands and it'll retain the results of those commands. This is similar to how files and many other things worked when you were working with f.readline().

When should I print versus return in a function?
You need to understand that print is only for printing to the screen and that you can actually both print and return a value. When you understand this, then you'll see that the question is kind of pointless. You use print when you want to print. You use return when you want to return.

Congratulations, Take a Test!

You are almost done with the first half of the book. The second half is where things get interesting. You will learn logic and be able to do useful things like make decisions.

Before you continue, I have a quiz for you. This quiz will be *very* hard because it requires you to fix someone else's code. When you are a programmer, you often have to deal with other programmers' code and also with their arrogance. Programmers will very frequently claim that their code is perfect.

These programmers are stupid people who care little for others. A good programmer assumes, like a good scientist, that there's always *some* probability their code is wrong. Good programmers start from the premise that their software is broken and then work to rule out all possible ways it could be wrong before finally admitting that maybe it really is the other guy's code.

In this exercise, you will practice dealing with a bad programmer by fixing a bad programmer's code. I have poorly copied Exercises 24 and 25 into a file and removed random characters and added flaws. Most of the errors are things Python will tell you, while some of them are math errors you should find. Others are formatting errors or spelling mistakes in the strings.

All these errors are very common mistakes all programmers make. Even experienced ones.

Your job in this exercise is to correct this file. Use all your skills to make this file better. Analyze it first, maybe printing it out to edit it like you would a school term paper. Fix each flaw and keep running it and fixing it until the script runs perfectly. Try not to get help, and if you get stuck, take a break and come back to it later.

Even if this takes days to do, bust through it and make it right.

Finally, the point of this exercise isn't to type it in but to fix an existing file. To do that, you must go to this site:

http://learnpythonthehardway.org/book/exercise26.txt

Copy-paste the code into a file named ex26.py. This is the only time you are allowed to copy-paste.

Common Student Questions

Do I have to import ex25.py or can I just remove the references to it?
You can do either. This file has the functions from ex25 though, so first go with removing references to it.

Can we run the code while we're fixing it?

You most certainly may. The computer is there to help, so use it as much as possible.

Memorizing Logic

Today is the day you start learning about logic. Up to this point, you have done everything you possibly can, reading and writing files to the Terminal, and have learned quite a lot of the math capabilities of Python.

From now on, you will be learning *logic*. You won't learn complex theories that academics love to study but just the simple basic logic that makes real programs work and that real programmers need every day.

Learning logic has to come after you do some memorization. I want you to do this exercise for an entire week. Do not falter. Even if you are bored out of your mind, keep doing it. This exercise has a set of logic tables you must memorize to make it easier for you to do the later exercises.

I'm warning you this won't be fun at first. It will be downright boring and tedious, but this is to teach you a very important skill you will need as a programmer. You *will* need to be able to memorize important concepts in your life. Most of these concepts will be exciting once you get them. You will struggle with them, like wrestling a squid, then one day *snap* you will understand it. All that work memorizing the basics pays off big later.

Here's a tip on how to memorize something without going insane: Do a tiny bit at a time throughout the day and mark down what you need to work on most. Do not try to sit down for two hours straight and memorize these tables. This won't work. Your brain will really only retain whatever you studied in the first 15 or 30 minutes anyway. Instead, what you should do is create a bunch of index cards with each column on the left on one side (True or False) and the column on the right on the back. You should then pull them out, see the "True or False," and be able to immediately say "True!" Keep practicing until you can do this.

Once you can do that, start writing out your own truth tables each night into a notebook. Do not just copy them. Try to do them from memory, and when you get stuck, glance quickly at the ones I have here to refresh your memory. Doing this will train your brain to remember the whole table.

Do not spend more than one week on this, because you will be applying it as you go.

The Truth Terms

In Python we have the following terms (characters and phrases) for determining if something is "True" or "False." Logic on a computer is all about seeing if some combination of these characters and some variables is True at that point in the program.

- and

- or

- not

- != (not equal)

- == (equal)

- >= (greater-than-equal)

- <= (less-than-equal)

- True

- False

You actually have run into these characters before, but maybe not the phrases. The phrases (and, or, not) actually work the way you expect them to, just like in English.

The Truth Tables

We will now use these characters to make the truth tables you need to memorize.

NOT	True?
not False	True
not True	False

OR	True?
True or False	True
True or True	True
False or True	True
False or False	False

AND	True?
True and False	False
True and True	True
False and True	False
False and False	False

NOT OR	True?
not (True or False)	False
not (True or True)	False
not (False or True)	False
not (False or False)	True

NOT AND	True?
not (True and False)	True
not (True and True)	False
not (False and True)	True
not (False and False)	True

!=	True?
1 != 0	True
1 != 1	False
0 != 1	True
0 != 0	False

==	True?
1 == 0	False
1 == 1	True
0 == 1	False
0 == 0	True

Now use these tables to write up your own cards and spend the week memorizing them. Remember though, there is no failing in this book, just trying as hard as you can each day, and then a *little* bit more.

Common Student Questions

Can't I just learn the concepts behind boolean algebra and not memorize this?
Sure, you can do that, but then you'll have to constantly go through the rules to boolean algebra while you code. If you memorize these first, it not only builds your memorization skills but also makes these operations natural. After that, the concept of boolean algebra is easy. But do whatever works for you.

Boolean Practice

The logic combinations you learned from the last exercise are called "boolean" logic expressions. Boolean logic is used *everywhere* in programming. They are essential fundamental parts of computation, and knowing them very well is akin to knowing your scales in music.

In this exercise, you will take the logic exercises you memorized and start trying them out in Python. Take each of these logic problems, and write out what you think the answer will be. In each case, it will be either True or False. Once you have the answers written down, you will start Python in your Terminal and type them in to confirm your answers.

1. True and True
2. False and True
3. 1 == 1 and 2 == 1
4. "test" == "test"
5. 1 == 1 or 2 != 1
6. True and 1 == 1
7. False and 0 != 0
8. True or 1 == 1
9. "test" == "testing"
10. 1 != 0 and 2 == 1
11. "test" != "testing"
12. "test" == 1
13. not (True and False)
14. not (1 == 1 and 0 != 1)
15. not (10 == 1 or 1000 == 1000)
16. not (1 != 10 or 3 == 4)
17. not ("testing" == "testing" and "Zed" == "Cool Guy")
18. 1 == 1 and not ("testing" == 1 or 1 == 0)
19. "chunky" == "bacon" and not (3 == 4 or 3 == 3)
20. 3 == 3 and not ("testing" == "testing" or "Python" == "Fun")

I will also give you a trick to help you figure out the more complicated ones toward the end.

Whenever you see these boolean logic statements, you can solve them easily by this simple process:

1.   Find an equality test (== or !=) and replace it with its truth.

2.   Find each and/or inside parentheses and solve those first.

3.   Find each not and invert it.

4.   Find any remaining and/or and solve it.

5.   When you are done, you should have `True` or `False`.

I will demonstrate with a variation on #20:

    3 != 4 and not ("testing" != "test" or "Python" == "Python")

Here's me going through each of the steps and showing you the translation until I've boiled it down to a single result:

1.   Solve each equality test:
    a.   3 != 4 is True: True and not ("testing" != "test" or "Python" == "Python")
    b.   "testing" != "test" is True: True and not (True or "Python" == "Python")
    c.   "Python" == "Python": True and not (True or True)

2.   Find each and/or in parentheses ():
    a.   (True or True) is True: True and not (True)

3.   Find each not and invert it:
    a.   not (True) is False: True and False

4.   Find any remaining and/or and solve them:
    a.   True and False is False

With that, we're done and know the result is False.

WARNING! The more complicated ones may seem *very* hard at first. You should be able to give a good first stab at solving them, but do not get discouraged. I'm just getting you primed for more of these "logic gymnastics" so that later cool stuff is much easier. Just stick with it, and keep track of what you get wrong, but do not worry that it's not getting in your head quite yet. It'll come.

What You Should See

After you have tried to guess at these, this is what your session with Python might look like:

```
$ python
Python 2.5.1 (r251:54863, Feb  6 2009, 19:02:12)
[GCC 4.0.1 (Apple Inc. build 5465)] on darwin
Type "help", "copyright", "credits" or "license" for more information.
>>> True and True
True
>>> 1 == 1 and 2 == 2
True
```

Study Drills

1. There are a lot of operators in Python similar to != and ==. Try to find out as many "equality operators" as you can. They should be like < or <=.

2. Write out the names of each of these equality operators. For example, I call != "not equal."

3. Play with the Python by typing out new boolean operators, and before you hit Enter, try to shout out what it is. Do not think about it—just name the first thing that comes to mind. Write it down, then hit Enter, and keep track of how many you get right and wrong.

4. Throw away the piece of paper from #3 so you do not accidentally try to use it later.

Common Student Questions

Why does "test" and "test" return "test" or 1 and 1 return 1 instead of True?
Python and many languages like it return one of the operands to their boolean expressions rather than just True or False. This means that if you did False and 1, then you get the first operand (False), but if you do True and 1, then you get the second (1). Play with this a bit.

Is there any difference between != and <>?
Python has deprecated <> in favor of !=, so use !=. Other than that, there should be no difference.

Isn't there a shortcut?
Yes. Any and expression that has a False is immediately False, so you can stop there. Any or expression that has a True is immediately True, so you can stop there. But make sure that you can process the whole expression, because later it becomes helpful.

What If

Here is the next script of Python you will enter, which introduces you to the if-statement. Type this in, make it run exactly right, and then we'll see if your practice has paid off.

ex29.py

```
1    people = 20
2    cats = 30
3    dogs = 15
4
5
6    if people < cats:
7        print "Too many cats! The world is doomed!"
8
9    if people > cats:
10       print "Not many cats! The world is saved!"
11
12   if people < dogs:
13       print "The world is drooled on!"
14
15   if people > dogs:
16       print "The world is dry!"
17
18
19   dogs += 5
20
21   if people >= dogs:
22       print "People are greater than or equal to dogs."
23
24   if people <= dogs:
25       print "People are less than or equal to dogs."
26
27
28   if people == dogs:
29       print "People are dogs."
```

What You Should See

Exercise 29 Session

```
$ python ex29.py
Too many cats! The world is doomed!
The world is dry!
People are greater than or equal to dogs.
People are less than or equal to dogs.
People are dogs.
```

Study Drills

In this Study Drill, try to guess what you think the if-statement is and what it does. Try to answer these questions in your own words before moving on to the next exercise:

1. What do you think the if does to the code under it?

2. Why does the code under the if need to be indented four spaces?

3. What happens if it isn't indented?

4. Can you put other boolean expressions from Exercise 27 in the if-statement? Try it.

5. What happens if you change the initial variables for people, cats, and dogs?

Common Student Questions

What does += mean?
The code x += 1 is the same as doing x = x + 1 but involves less typing. You can call this the "increment by" operator. The same goes for -= and many other expressions you'll learn later.

Else and If

In the last exercise, you worked out some if-statements and then tried to guess what they are and how they work. Before you learn more, I'll explain what everything is by answering the questions you had from the Study Drills. You did the Study Drills, right?

1. What do you think the if does to the code under it? An if-statement creates what is called a "branch" in the code. It's kind of like those choose-your-own-adventure books where you are asked to turn to one page if you make one choice and another if you go a different direction. The if-statement tells your script, "If this boolean expression is True, then run the code under it, otherwise skip it."

2. Why does the code under the if need to be indented four spaces? A colon at the end of a line is how you tell Python you are going to create a new "block" of code, and then indenting four spaces tells Python what lines of code are in that block. This is *exactly* the same thing you did when you made functions in the first half of the book.

3. What happens if it isn't indented? If it isn't indented, you will most likely create a Python error. Python expects you to indent *something* after you end a line with a : (colon).

4. Can you put other boolean expressions from Exercise 27 in the if-statement? Try it. Yes, you can, and they can be as complex as you like, although really complex things generally are bad style.

5. What happens if you change the initial values for people, cats, and dogs? Because you are comparing numbers, if you change the numbers, different if-statements will evaluate to True, and the blocks of code under them will run. Go back and put different numbers in and see if you can figure out in your head what blocks of code will run.

Compare my answers to your answers, and make sure you *really* understand the concept of a "block" of code. This is important for when you do the next exercise, where you write all the parts of if-statements that you can use.

Type this one in and make it work too.

ex30.py

```
1   people = 30
2   cars = 40
3   buses = 15
4
5
6   if cars > people:
7       print "We should take the cars."
8   elif cars < people:
```

```
9          print "We should not take the cars."
10   else:
11          print "We can't decide."
12
13   if buses > cars:
14          print "That's too many buses."
15   elif buses < cars:
16          print "Maybe we could take the buses."
17   else:
18          print "We still can't decide."
19
20   if people > buses:
21          print "Alright, let's just take the buses."
22   else:
23          print "Fine, let's stay home then."
```

What You Should See

Exercise 30 Session

```
$ python ex30.py
We should take the cars.
Maybe we could take the buses.
Alright, let's just take the buses.
```

Study Drills

1. Try to guess what elif and else are doing.

2. Change the numbers of cars, people, and buses, and then trace through each if-statement to see what will be printed.

3. Try some more complex boolean expressions like cars > people and buses < cars.

4. Above each line, write an English description of what the line does.

Common Student Questions

What happens if multiple elif blocks are True?
Python starts at the top and runs the first block that is True, so it will run only the first one.

Making Decisions

In the first half of this book, you mostly just printed out things called functions, but everything was basically in a straight line. Your scripts ran starting at the top and went to the bottom where they ended. If you made a function, you could run that function later, but it still didn't have the kind of branching you need to really make decisions. Now that you have if, else, and elif, you can start to make scripts that decide things.

In the last script you wrote out a simple set of tests asking some questions. In this script you will ask the user questions and make decisions based on their answers. Write this script, and then play with it quite a lot to figure it out.

ex31.py

```
1    print "You enter a dark room with two doors.  Do you go through door #1 or door #2?"
2
3    door = raw_input("> ")
4
5    if door == "1":
6        print "There's a giant bear here eating a cheese cake.  What do you do?"
7        print "1. Take the cake."
8        print "2. Scream at the bear."
9
10       bear = raw_input("> ")
11
12       if bear == "1":
13           print "The bear eats your face off.  Good job!"
14       elif bear == "2":
15           print "The bear eats your legs off.  Good job!"
16       else:
17           print "Well, doing %s is probably better.  Bear runs away." % bear
18
19   elif door == "2":
20       print "You stare into the endless abyss at Cthulhu's retina."
21       print "1. Blueberries."
22       print "2. Yellow jacket clothespins."
23       print "3. Understanding revolvers yelling melodies."
24
25       insanity = raw_input("> ")
26
27       if insanity == "1" or insanity == "2":
28           print "Your body survives powered by a mind of jello.  Good job!"
29       else:
30           print "The insanity rots your eyes into a pool of muck.  Good job!"
31
32   else:
33       print "You stumble around and fall on a knife and die.  Good job!"
```

A key point here is that you are now putting the if-statements *inside* if-statements as code that can run. This is very powerful and can be used to create "nested" decisions, where one branch leads to another and another.

Make sure you understand this concept of if-statements inside if-statements. In fact, do the Study Drills to really nail it.

What You Should See

Here is me playing this little adventure game. I do not do so well.

```
$ python ex31.py
You enter a dark room with two doors.  Do you go through door #1 or door #2?
> 1
There's a giant bear here eating a cheese cake.  What do you do?
1. Take the cake.
2. Scream at the bear.
> 2
The bear eats your legs off.  Good job!
```

Study Drills

Make new parts of the game and change what decisions people can make. Expand the game out as much as you can before it gets ridiculous.

Common Student Questions

Can you replace elif with a sequence of if/else combinations?
You can in some situations, but it depends on how each if/else is written. It also means that Python will check *every* if/else combination, rather than just the first false ones, like it would with if/elif/else. Try to make some of these to figure out the differences.

How do I tell if a number is between a range of numbers?
You have two options: Use 0 < x < 10 or 1 <= x < 10, which is classic notation, or use x in range(1, 10).

What if I wanted more options in the if/elif/else blocks?
Easy, just add more elif blocks for each possible choice.

Loops and Lists

You should now be able to do some programs that are much more interesting. If you have been keeping up, you should realize that now you can combine all the other things you have learned with if-statements and boolean expressions to make your programs do smart things.

However, programs also need to do repetitive things very quickly. We are going to use a for-loop in this exercise to build and print various lists. When you do the exercise, you will start to figure out what they are. I won't tell you right now. You have to figure it out.

Before you can use a for-loop, you need a way to *store* the results of loops somewhere. The best way to do this is with a list. A list is exactly what its name says—a container of things that are organized in order. It's not complicated; you just have to learn a new syntax. First, there's how you make a list:

```
hairs = ['brown', 'blond', 'red']
eyes = ['brown', 'blue', 'green']
weights = [1, 2, 3, 4]
```

What you do is start the list with the [(left bracket), which "opens" the list. Then you put each item you want in the list separated by commas, just like when you did function arguments. Lastly you end the list with a] (right bracket) to indicate that it's over. Python then takes this list and all its contents and assigns them to the variable.

WARNING! This is where things get tricky for people who can't program. Your brain has been taught that the world is flat. Remember in the last exercise where you put if-statements inside if-statements? That probably made your brain hurt because most people do not ponder how to "nest" things inside things. In programming, this is all over the place. You will find functions that call other functions that have if-statements including lists with lists inside lists. If you see a structure like this that you can't figure out, take out a pencil and paper and break it down manually bit by bit until you understand it.

We now will build some lists using some loops and print them out:

ex32.py

```
1    the_count = [1, 2, 3, 4, 5]
2    fruits = ['apples', 'oranges', 'pears', 'apricots']
3    change = [1, 'pennies', 2, 'dimes', 3, 'quarters']
4
5    # this first kind of for-loop goes through a list
```

```
6    for number in the_count:
7        print "This is count %d" % number
8
9    # same as above
10   for fruit in fruits:
11       print "A fruit of type: %s" % fruit
12
13   # also we can go through mixed lists too
14   # notice we have to use %r since we don't know what's in it
15   for i in change:
16       print "I got %r" % i
17
18   # we can also build lists, first start with an empty one
19   elements = []
20
21   # then use the range function to do 0 to 5 counts
22   for i in range(0, 6):
23       print "Adding %d to the list." % i
24       # append is a function that lists understand
25       elements.append(i)
26
27   # now we can print them out too
28   for i in elements:
29       print "Element was: %d" % i
```

What You Should See

```
$ python ex32.py
This is count 1
This is count 2
This is count 3
This is count 4
This is count 5
A fruit of type: apples
A fruit of type: oranges
A fruit of type: pears
A fruit of type: apricots
I got 1
I got 'pennies'
I got 2
I got 'dimes'
I got 3
I got 'quarters'
Adding 0 to the list.
Adding 1 to the list.
Adding 2 to the list.
Adding 3 to the list.
Adding 4 to the list.
```

```
Adding 5 to the list.
Element was: 0
Element was: 1
Element was: 2
Element was: 3
Element was: 4
Element was: 5
```

Study Drills

1. Take a look at how you used range. Look up the range function to understand it.

2. Could you have avoided that for-loop entirely on line 22 and just assigned range(0,6) directly to elements?

3. Find the Python documentation on lists and read about them. What other operations can you do to lists besides append?

Common Student Questions

How do you make a two-dimensional (2D) list?
That's a list in a list like this: [[1,2,3],[4,5,6]].

Aren't lists and arrays the same thing?
It depends on the language and the implementation. In classic terms, lists are very different from arrays because of how they're implemented. In Ruby, lists are referred to as arrays. In Python, they're referred to as lists. Just call these lists for now, since that's what Python calls them.

How come a for-loop can use variables that aren't defined yet?
It defines that variable, initializing it to the current element of the loop iteration, each time through.

Why does for i in range(1, 3): only loop two times instead of three times?
The range() function only does numbers from the first to the last, *not including the last*. So it stops at two, not three, in the above. This turns out to be the most common way to do this kind of loop.

What does elements.append() do?
It simply appends to the end of the list. Open up the Python shell and try a few examples with a list you make. Any time you run into things like this, always try to play with them interactively in the Python shell.

While-Loops

Now to totally blow your mind with a new loop—the while-loop. A while-loop will keep executing the code block under it as long as a boolean expression is True.

Wait, you have been keeping up with the terminology, right? That if we write a line and end it with a : (colon), then that tells Python to start a new block of code? Then we indent and that's the new code. This is all about structuring your programs so that Python knows what you mean. If you do not get that idea, then go back and do some more work with if-statements, functions, and the for-loop until you get it.

Later on, we'll have some exercises that will train your brain to read these structures, similar to how we burned boolean expressions into your brain.

Back to while-loops. What they do is simply do a test like an if-statement, but instead of running the code block *once*, they jump back to the "top" where the while is and repeat. It keeps doing this until the expression is False.

Here's the problem with while-loops: Sometimes they do not stop. This is great if your intention is to just keep looping until the end of the universe. Otherwise you almost always want your loops to end eventually.

To avoid these problems, there's some rules to follow:

1. Make sure that you use while-loops sparingly. Usually a for-loop is better.

2. Review your while statements and make sure that the thing you are testing will become False at some point.

3. When in doubt, print out your test variable at the top and bottom of the while-loop to see what it's doing.

In this exercise, you will learn the while-loop by doing the above three things:

ex33.py

```
1    i = 0
2    numbers = []
3
4    while i < 6:
5        print "At the top i is %d" % i
6        numbers.append(i)
7
8        i = i + 1
9        print "Numbers now: ", numbers
```

```
10        print "At the bottom i is %d" % i
11
12
13    print "The numbers: "
14
15    for num in numbers:
16        print num
```

What You Should See

```
$ python ex33.py
At the top i is 0
Numbers now:  [0]
At the bottom i is 1
At the top i is 1
Numbers now:  [0, 1]
At the bottom i is 2
At the top i is 2
Numbers now:  [0, 1, 2]
At the bottom i is 3
At the top i is 3
Numbers now:  [0, 1, 2, 3]
At the bottom i is 4
At the top i is 4
Numbers now:  [0, 1, 2, 3, 4]
At the bottom i is 5
At the top i is 5
Numbers now:  [0, 1, 2, 3, 4, 5]
At the bottom i is 6
The numbers:
0
1
2
3
4
5
```

Study Drills

1. Convert this while-loop to a function that you can call, and replace 6 in the test ($i < 6$) with a variable.

2. Now use this function to rewrite the script to try different numbers.

3. Add another variable to the function arguments that you can pass in that lets you change the + 1 on line 8, so you can change how much it increments by.

4. Rewrite the script again to use this function to see what effect that has.

5. Now, write it to use for-loops and range instead. Do you need the incrementor in the middle anymore? What happens if you do not get rid of it?

If at any time that you are doing this it goes crazy (it probably will), just hold down CTRL and hit c (CTRL-c) and the program will abort.

Common Student Questions

What's the difference between a for-loop and a while-loop?
A for-loop can only iterate (loop) "over" collections of things. A while-loop can do any kind of iteration (looping) you want. However, while-loops are harder to get right and you normally can get many things done with for-loops.

Loops are hard. How do I figure them out?
The main reason people don't understand loops is because they can't follow the "jumping" that the code does. When a loop runs, it goes through its block of code, and at the end it jumps back to the top. To visualize this, put print statements all over the loop, printing out where in the loop Python is running and what the variables are set to at those points. Put prints before the loop, at the top of the loop, in the middle, and at the bottom. Study the output and try to understand the jumping that's going on.

Accessing Elements of Lists

Lists are pretty useful, but only if you can get at the things inside them. You can already go through the elements of a list in order, but what if you want, say, the fifth element? You need to know how to access the elements of a list. Here's how you would access the *first* element of a list:

```
animals = ['bear', 'tiger', 'penguin', 'zebra']
bear = animals[0]
```

You take a list of animals, and then you get the first (1st) one using 0?! How does that work? Because of the way math works, Python start its lists at 0 rather than 1. It seems weird, but there's many advantages to this, even though it is mostly arbitrary.

The best way to explain why is by showing you the difference between how you use numbers and how programmers use numbers.

Imagine you are watching the four animals in our list above (['bear', 'tiger', 'penguin', 'zebra']) run in a race. They win in the *order* we have them in this list. The race was really exciting because the animals didn't eat each other and somehow managed to run a race. Your friend, however, shows up late and wants to know who won. Does your friend say, "Hey, who came in *zeroth*?" No, he says, "Hey, who came in *first*?"

This is because the *order* of the animals is important. You can't have the second animal without the first (1st) animal, and you can't have the third without the second. It's also impossible to have a "zeroth" animal since zero means nothing. How can you have a nothing win a race? It just doesn't make sense. We call these kinds of numbers "ordinal" numbers, because they indicate an ordering of things.

Programmers, however, can't think this way because they can pick any element out of a list at any point. To programmers, the above list is more like a deck of cards. If they want the tiger, they grab it. If they want the zebra, they can take it too. This need to pull elements out of lists at random means that they need a way to indicate elements consistently by an address, or an "index," and the best way to do that is to start the indices at 0. Trust me on this: the math is *way* easier for these kinds of accesses. This kind of number is a "cardinal" number and means you can pick at random, so there needs to be a 0 element.

How does this help you work with lists? Simply put, every time you say to yourself, "I want the third animal," you translate this "ordinal" number to a "cardinal" number by subtracting 1. The "third" animal is at index 2 and is the penguin. You have to do this because you have spent your whole life using ordinal numbers, and now you have to think in cardinal. Just subtract 1 and you will be good.

Remember: ordinal == ordered, 1st; cardinal == cards at random, 0.

Let's practice this. Take this list of animals, and follow the exercises where I tell you to write down what animal you get for that ordinal or cardinal number. Remember, if I say "first," "second," and so on, then I'm using ordinal, so subtract 1. If I give you cardinals (0, 1, 2), then use it directly.

```
animals = ['bear', 'python', 'peacock', 'kangaroo', 'whale', 'platypus']
```

1.   The animal at 1.

2.   The third animal.

3.   The first animal.

4.   The animal at 3.

5.   The fifth animal.

6.   The animal at 2.

7.   The sixth animal.

8.   The animal at 4.

For each of these, write out a full sentence of the form: "The first animal is at 0 and is a bear." Then say it backward, "The animal at 0 is the first animal and is a bear." Use your Python to check your answers.

Study Drills

1.   Read about ordinal and cardinal numbers online.

2.   With what you know of the difference between these types of numbers, can you explain why the year 2010 in "January 1, 2010," really is 2010 and not 2009? (Hint: you can't pick years at random.)

3.   Write some more lists and work out similar indexes until you can translate them.

4.   Use Python to check your answers to this as well.

WARNING! Programmers will tell you to read this guy named "Dijkstra" on this subject. I recommend you avoid his writings on this unless you enjoy being yelled at by someone who stopped programming at the same time programming started.

Branches and Functions

You have learned to do if-statements, functions, and lists. Now it's time to bend your mind. Type this in, and see if you can figure out what it's doing.

ex35.py

```
1    from sys import exit
2
3    def gold_room():
4        print "This room is full of gold.  How much do you take?"
5
6        next = raw_input("> ")
7        if "0" in next or "1" in next:
8            how_much = int(next)
9        else:
10           dead("Man, learn to type a number.")
11
12       if how_much < 50:
13           print "Nice, you're not greedy, you win!"
14           exit(0)
15       else:
16           dead("You greedy bastard!")
17
18
19   def bear_room():
20       print "There is a bear here."
21       print "The bear has a bunch of honey."
22       print "The fat bear is in front of another door."
23       print "How are you going to move the bear?"
24       bear_moved = False
25
26       while True:
27           next = raw_input("> ")
28
29           if next == "take honey":
30               dead("The bear looks at you then slaps your face off.")
31           elif next == "taunt bear" and not bear_moved:
32               print "The bear has moved from the door. You can go through it now."
33               bear_moved = True
34           elif next == "taunt bear" and bear_moved:
35               dead("The bear gets pissed off and chews your leg off.")
36           elif next == "open door" and bear_moved:
37               gold_room()
38           else:
39               print "I got no idea what that means."
40
41
```

```
42   def cthulhu_room():
43       print "Here you see the great evil Cthulhu."
44       print "He, it, whatever stares at you and you go insane."
45       print "Do you flee for your life or eat your head?"
46
47       next = raw_input("> ")
48
49       if "flee" in next:
50           start()
51       elif "head" in next:
52           dead("Well that was tasty!")
53       else:
54           cthulhu_room()
55
56
57   def dead(why):
58       print why, "Good job!"
59       exit(0)
60
61   def start():
62       print "You are in a dark room."
63       print "There is a door to your right and left."
64       print "Which one do you take?"
65
66       next = raw_input("> ")
67
68       if next == "left":
69           bear_room()
70       elif next == "right":
71           cthulhu_room()
72       else:
73           dead("You stumble around the room until you starve.")
74
75
76   start()
```

What You Should See

Here's me playing the game:

```
$ python ex35.py
You are in a dark room.
There is a door to your right and left.
Which one do you take?
> left
There is a bear here.
The bear has a bunch of honey.
```

The fat bear is in front of another door.
How are you going to move the bear?
> taunt bear
The bear has moved from the door. You can go through it now.
> open door
This room is full of gold. How much do you take?
> 1000
You greedy bastard! Good job!

Study Drills

1.   Draw a map of the game and how you flow through it.

2.   Fix all your mistakes, including spelling mistakes.

3.   Write comments for the functions you do not understand. Remember doc comments?

4.   Add more to the game. What can you do to both simplify and expand it?

5.   The gold_room has a weird way of getting you to type a number. What are all the bugs in this way of doing it? Can you make it better than just checking if "1" or "0" are in the number? Look at how int() works for clues.

Common Student Questions

Help! How does this program work!?
Any time you get stuck understanding a piece of software, simply write an English comment above *every* line, explaining what it does. As you go through doing this, correct comments that aren't right, based on new information. Then when you're done, try to either diagram how it works or write a paragraph or two describing it. If you do that, you'll get it.

Why are you doing while True:?
That makes an infinite loop.

What does exit(0) do?
On many operating systems, a program can abort with exit(0), and the number passed in will indicate an error or not. If you do exit(1), then it will be an error, but exit(0) will be a good exit. The reason it's backward from normal boolean logic (with 0==False) is that you can use different numbers to indicate different error results. You can do exit(100) for a different error result than exit(2) or exit(1).

Why is raw_input() sometimes written as raw_input('> ')?
The parameter to raw_input is a string that it should print as a prompt before getting the user's input.

Designing and Debugging

Now that you know if-statements, I'm going to give you some rules for for-loops and while-loops that will keep you out of trouble. I'm also going to give you some tips on debugging so that you can figure out problems with your program. Finally, you are going to design a similar little game as in the last exercise but with a slight twist.

Rules for If-Statements

1. Every if-statement must have an else.

2. If this else should never be run because it doesn't make sense, then you must use a die function in the else that prints out an error message and dies, just like we did in the last exercise. This will find *many* errors.

3. Never nest if-statements more than two deep and always try to do them one deep. This means if you put an if in an if, then you should be looking to move that second if into another function.

4. Treat if-statements like paragraphs, where each if, elif, else grouping is like a set of sentences. Put blank lines before and after.

5. Your boolean tests should be simple. If they are complex, move their calculations to variables earlier in your function and use a good name for the variable.

If you follow these simple rules, you will start writing better code than most programmers. Go back to the last exercise and see if I followed all these rules. If not, fix it.

WARNING! Never be a slave to the rules in real life. For training purposes, you need to follow these rules to make your mind strong, but in real life sometimes these rules are just stupid. If you think a rule is stupid, try not using it.

Rules for Loops

1. Use a while-loop only to loop forever, and that means probably never. This only applies to Python; other languages are different.

2. Use a for-loop for all other kinds of looping, especially if there is a fixed or limited number of things to loop over.

Tips for Debugging

1.   Do not use a "debugger." A debugger is like doing a full-body scan on a sick person. You do not get any specific useful information, and you find a whole lot of information that doesn't help and is just confusing.

2.   The best way to debug a program is to use `print` to print out the values of variables at points in the program to see where they go wrong.

3.   Make sure parts of your programs work as you work on them. Do not write massive files of code before you try to run them. Code a little, run a little, fix a little.

Homework

Now write a similar game to the one that I created in the last exercise. It can be any kind of game you want in the same flavor. Spend a week on it, making it as interesting as possible. For Study Drills, use lists, functions, and modules (remember those from Exercise 13?) as much as possible, and find as many new pieces of Python as you can to make the game work.

However, before you start coding, you must write up a map for your game. Create the rooms, monsters, and traps that the player must go through on paper before you code.

Once you have your map, try to code it up. If you find problems with the map, then adjust it and make the code match.

One final word of advice: All programmers become paralyzed by irrational fear starting a new large project. They procrastinate to avoid contronting this fear and end up not getting their program working or even started. I do this. Everyone does this. The best way to avoid this is to make a list of things you should do and then do them one at a time.

Just start doing it, do a small version, make it bigger, keep a list of things to do, and do them.

Symbol Review

I t's time to review the symbols and Python words you know and try to pick up a few more for the next few lessons. What I've done here is written out all the Python symbols and keywords that are important to know.

In this lesson take each keyword and first try to write out what it does from memory. Next, search online for it and see what it really does. It may be hard because some of these are going to be impossible to search for, but keep trying.

If you get one of these wrong from memory, write up an index card with the correct definition, and try to "correct" your memory. If you just didn't know about it, write it down, and save it for later.

Finally, use each of these in a small Python program, or as many as you can get done. The key here is to find out what the symbol does, make sure you got it right, correct it if you do not, then use it to lock it in.

Keywords

- and
- del
- from
- not
- while
- as
- elif
- global
- or
- with
- assert
- else
- if

- pass
- yield
- break
- except
- import
- print
- class
- exec
- in
- raise
- continue
- finally
- is
- return
- def
- for
- lambda
- try

Data Types

For data types, write out what makes up each one. For example, with strings write out how you create a string. For numbers, write out a few numbers.

- True
- False
- None
- strings
- numbers
- floats
- lists

String Escape Sequences

For string escape sequences, use them in strings to make sure they do what you think they do.

- \\
- \'
- \"
- \a
- \b
- \f
- \n
- \r
- \t
- \v

String Formats

Same thing for string formats: use them in some strings to know what they do.

- %d
- %i
- %o
- %u
- %x
- %X
- %e
- %E
- %f
- %F
- %g
- %G

- %c
- %r
- %s
- %%

Operators

Some of these may be unfamiliar to you, but look them up anyway. Find out what they do, and if you still can't figure it out, save it for later.

- +
- −
- *
- **
- /
- //
- %
- <
- >
- <=
- >=
- ==
- !=
- <>
- ( )
- [ ]
- { }
- @
- ,
- :

- .
- =
- ;
- +=
- -=
- *=
- /=
- //=
- %=
- **=

Spend about a week on this, but if you finish faster that's great. The point is to try to get coverage on all these symbols and make sure they are locked in your head. What's also important is to find out what you *do not* know so you can fix it later.

Reading Code

Now go find some Python code to read. You should be reading any Python code you can and trying to steal ideas that you find. You actually should have enough knowledge to be able to read but maybe not understand what the code does. What I'm going to teach you in this lesson is how to apply things you have learned to understand other people's code.

First, print out the code you want to understand. Yes, print it out, because your eyes and brain are more used to reading paper than computer screens. Make sure you only print a few pages at a time.

Second, go through your printout and make note of the following:

1. Functions and what they do.
2. Where each variable is first given a value.
3. Any variables with the same names in different parts of the program. These may be trouble later.
4. Any `if-statements` without `else` clauses. Are they right?
5. Any `while-loops` that might not end.
6. Finally, any parts of code that you can't understand for whatever reason.

Third, once you have all this marked up, try to explain it to yourself by writing comments as you go. Explain the functions, how they are used, what variables are involved, and anything you can to figure this code out.

Lastly, on all the difficult parts, trace the values of each variable line by line, function by function. In fact, do another printout and write in the margin the value of each variable that you need to "trace."

Once you have a good idea of what the code does, go back to the computer and read it again to see if you find new things. Keep finding more code and doing this until you do not need the printouts anymore.

Study Drills

1. Find out what a "flow chart" is and write a few.

2. If you find errors in code you are reading, try to fix them and send the author your changes.

3. Another technique for when you are not using paper is to put # comments with your notes in the code. Sometimes, these could become the actual comments to help the next person.

Common Student Questions

What's the difference between %d and %i formatting?
Shouldn't be any difference, other than the fact that people use %d more due to historical reasons.

How would I search for these things online?
Simply put "python" before anything you want to find. For example, to find `yield` do `python yield`.

Doing Things to Lists

You have learned about lists. When you learned about while-loops, you "appended" numbers to the end of a list and printed them out. There were also Study Drills where you were supposed to find all the other things you can do to lists in the Python documentation. That was a while back, so go find in the book where you did that and review if you do not know what I'm talking about.

Found it? Remember it? Good. When you did this, you had a list and you "called" the function append on it. However, you may not really understand what's going on, so let's see what we can do to lists.

When you type Python code that reads mystuff.append('hello'), you are actually setting off a chain of events inside Python to cause something to happen to the mystuff list. Here's how it works:

1. Python sees you mentioned mystuff and looks up that variable. It might have to look backward to see if you created it with =, and look and see if it is a function argument or a global variable. Either way, it has to find the mystuff first.

2. Once it finds mystuff it then hits the . (period) operator and starts to look at *variables* that are a part of mystuff. Since mystuff is a list, it knows that mystuff has a bunch of functions.

3. It then hits append and compares the name "append" to all the ones that mystuff says it owns. If append is in there (it is), then it grabs *that* to use.

4. Next Python sees the ((parenthesis) and realizes, "Oh hey, this should be a function." At this point it *calls* (a.k.a. runs, executes) the function just like normally, but instead it calls the function with an *extra* argument.

5. That *extra* argument is . . . mystuff! I know, weird, right? But that's how Python works so it's best to just remember it and assume that's alright. What happens then, at the end of all this, is a function call that looks like append(mystuff, 'hello') instead of what you read, which is mystuff.append('hello').

For the most part you do not have to know that this is going on, but it helps when you get error messages from Python like this:

```
$ python
Python 2.6.5 (r265:79063, Apr 16 2010, 13:57:41)
[GCC 4.4.3] on linux2
Type "help", "copyright", "credits" or "license" for more information.
>>> class Thing(object):
```

```
...        def test(hi):
...              print "hi"
...
>>> a = Thing()
>>> a.test("hello")
Traceback (most recent call last):
  File "<stdin>", line 1, in <module>
TypeError: test() takes exactly 1 argument (2 given)
>>>
```

What was all that? Well, this is me typing into the Python shell and showing you some magic. You haven't seen class yet but we'll get into that later. For now, you see how Python said test() takes exactly 1 argument (2 given). If you see this, it means that Python changed a.test("hello") to test(a, "hello") and that somewhere someone messed up and didn't add the argument for a.

That might be a lot to take in, but we're going to spend a few exercises getting this concept firm in your brain. To kick things off, here's an exercise that mixes strings and lists for all kinds of fun.

ex38.py

```
1   ten_things = "Apples Oranges Crows Telephone Light Sugar"
2
3   print "Wait there's not 10 things in that list, let's fix that."
4
5   stuff = ten_things.split(' ')
6   more_stuff = ["Day", "Night", "Song", "Frisbee", "Corn", "Banana", "Girl", "Boy"]
7
8   while len(stuff) != 10:
9       next_one = more_stuff.pop()
10      print "Adding: ", next_one
11      stuff.append(next_one)
12      print "There's %d items now." % len(stuff)
13
14  print "There we go: ", stuff
15
16  print "Let's do some things with stuff."
17
18  print stuff[1]
19  print stuff[-1] # whoa! fancy
20  print stuff.pop()
21  print ' '.join(stuff) # what? cool!
22  print '#'.join(stuff[3:5]) # super stellar!
```

What You Should See

```
$ python ex38.py
Wait there's not 10 things in that list, let's fix that.
```

```
Adding:  Boy
There's 7 items now.
Adding:  Girl
There's 8 items now.
Adding:  Banana
There's 9 items now.
Adding:  Corn
There's 10 items now.
There we go: ['Apples', 'Oranges', 'Crows', 'Telephone', 'Light', 'Sugar',
'Boy', 'Girl', 'Banana', 'Corn']
Let's do some things with stuff.
Oranges
Corn
Corn
Apples Oranges Crows Telephone Light Sugar Boy Girl Banana
Telephone#Light
```

Study Drills

1. Take each function that is called, and go through the steps outlined above to translate them to what Python does. For example, ' '.join(things) is join(' ', things).

2. Translate these two ways to view the function calls. For example, ' '.join(things) reads as, "Join things with ' ' between them." Meanwhile, join(' ', things) means, "Call join with ' ' and things." Understand how they are really the same thing.

3. Go read about "object-oriented programming" online. Confused? I was too. Do not worry. You will learn enough to be dangerous, and you can slowly learn more later.

4. Read up on what a "class" is in Python. *Do not read about how other languages use the word "class."* That will only mess you up.

5. What's the relationship between dir(something) and the "class" of something?

6. If you do not have any idea what I'm talking about, do not worry. Programmers like to feel smart, so they invented object-oriented programming, named it OOP, and then used it way too much. If you think that's hard, you should try to use "functional programming."

Common Student Questions

Didn't you say to not use while-loops?
Yes, so just remember sometimes you can break the rules if you have a good reason. Only idiots are slaves to rules all the time.

What does stuff[3:5] do?
That's getting a "slice" from the stuff list that is from element 3 to element 4, meaning it does *not* include element 5. It's similar to how range(3,5) would work.

Why does join(' ', stuff) not work?
The way the documentation for join is written doesn't make sense. It does not work like that and is instead a method you call on the *inserted* string to put between the list to be joined. Rewrite it like ' '.join(stuff).

Dictionaries, Oh Lovely Dictionaries

N ow I have to hurt you with another container you can use, because once you learn this container, a massive world of ultra-cool will be yours. It is the most useful container ever: the dictionary.

Python calls them "dicts." Other languages call them "hashes." I tend to use both names, but it doesn't matter. What does matter is what they do when compared to lists. You see, a list lets you do this:

```
>>> things = ['a', 'b', 'c', 'd']
>>> print things[1]
b
>>> things[1] = 'z'
>>> print things[1]
z
>>> print things
['a', 'z', 'c', 'd']
>>>
```

You can use numbers to "index" into a list, meaning you can use numbers to find out what's in lists. You should know this about lists by now, but make sure you understand that you can *only* use numbers to get items out of a list.

What a dict does is let you use *anything*, not just numbers. Yes, a dict associates one thing to another, no matter what it is. Take a look:

```
>>> stuff = {'name': 'Zed', 'age': 36, 'height': 6*12+2}
>>> print stuff['name']
Zed
>>> print stuff['age']
36
>>> print stuff['height']
74
>>> stuff['city'] = "San Francisco"
>>> print stuff['city']
San Francisco
>>>
```

You will see that instead of just numbers we're using strings to say what we want from the stuff dictionary. We can also put new things into the dictionary with strings. It doesn't have to be strings though. We can also do this:

```
>>> stuff[1] = "Wow"
>>> stuff[2] = "Neato"
>>> print stuff[1]
Wow
>>> print stuff[2]
Neato
>>> print stuff
{'city': 'San Francisco', 2: 'Neato',
    'name': 'Zed', 1: 'Wow', 'age': 36,
    'height': 74}
>>>
```

In this code I used numbers, and then you can see there are numbers and strings as keys in the dict when I print it. I could use anything—well, almost, but just pretend you can use anything for now.

Of course, a dictionary that you can only put things in is pretty stupid, so here's how you delete things, with the del keyword:

```
>>> del stuff['city']
>>> del stuff[1]
>>> del stuff[2]
>>> stuff
{'name': 'Zed', 'age': 36, 'height': 74}
>>>
```

We'll now do an exercise that you *must* study very carefully. I want you to type this exercise in and try to understand what's going on. Take note of when I put things in a dict, get from them, and all the operations I use here.

ex39.py

```
1    # create a mapping of state to abbreviation
2    states = {
3        'Oregon': 'OR',
4        'Florida': 'FL',
5        'California': 'CA',
6        'New York': 'NY',
7        'Michigan': 'MI'
8    }
9
10   # create a basic set of states and some cities in them
11   cities = {
12       'CA': 'San Francisco',
13       'MI': 'Detroit',
14       'FL': 'Jacksonville'
15   }
16
17   # add some more cities
18   cities['NY'] = 'New York'
19   cities['OR'] = 'Portland'
```

```
20
21   # print out some cities
22   print '-' * 10
23   print "NY State has: ", cities['NY']
24   print "OR State has: ", cities['OR']
25
26   # print some states
27   print '-' * 10
28   print "Michigan's abbreviation is: ", states['Michigan']
29   print "Florida's abbreviation is: ", states['Florida']
30
31   # do it by using the state then cities dict
32   print '-' * 10
33   print "Michigan has: ", cities[states['Michigan']]
34   print "Florida has: ", cities[states['Florida']]
35
36   # print every state abbreviation
37   print '-' * 10
38   for state, abbrev in states.items():
39       print "%s is abbreviated %s" % (state, abbrev)
40
41   # print every city in state
42   print '-' * 10
43   for abbrev, city in cities.items():
44       print "%s has the city %s" % (abbrev, city)
45
46   # now do both at the same time
47   print '-' * 10
48   for state, abbrev in states.items():
49       print "%s state is abbreviated %s and has city %s" % (
50           state, abbrev, cities[abbrev])
51
52   print '-' * 10
53   # safely get an abbreviation by state that might not be there
54   state = states.get('Texas', None)
55
56   if not state:
57       print "Sorry, no Texas."
58
59   # get a city with a default value
60   city = cities.get('TX', 'Does Not Exist')
61   print "The city for the state 'TX' is: %s" % city
```

What You Should See

```
$ python ex39.py
----------
NY State has:  New York
```

```
OR State has:  Portland
----------
Michigan's abbreviation is:  MI
Florida's abbreviation is:  FL
----------
Michigan has:  Detroit
Florida has:  Jacksonville
----------
California is abbreviated CA
Michigan is abbreviated MI
New York is abbreviated NY
Florida is abbreviated FL
Oregon is abbreviated OR
----------
FL has the city Jacksonville
CA has the city San Francisco
MI has the city Detroit
OR has the city Portland
NY has the city New York
----------
California state is abbreviated CA and has city San Francisco
Michigan state is abbreviated MI and has city Detroit
New York state is abbreviated NY and has city New York
Florida state is abbreviated FL and has city Jacksonville
Oregon state is abbreviated OR and has city Portland
----------
Sorry, no Texas.
The city for the state 'TX' is: Does Not Exist
```

Study Drills

1. Do this same kind of mapping with cities and states/regions in your country or in some other country.

2. Go find the Python documentation for dictionaries (a.k.a. dicts, dict), and try to do even more things to them.

3. Find out what you *can't* do with dictionaries. A big limitation is that they do not have order, so try playing with that.

Common Student Questions

What the difference between a list and a dictionary?
A list is for an ordered list of items. A dictionary (or dict) is for matching some items (called "keys") to other items (called "values").

What would I use a dictionary for?
Use it any time you have to take one value and "look up" another value. In fact, you could call dictionaries "look up tables."

What would I use a list for?
A list is for any sequence of things that need to go in order, and you only need to look them up by a numeric index.

What if I need a dictionary, but I need it to be in order?
Take a look at the `collections.OrderedDict` data structure in Python. Search for it online to find the documentation.

Modules, Classes, and Objects

Python is something called an "object-oriented programming language." What this means is there's a construct in Python called a class that lets you structure your software in a particular way. Using classes, you can add consistency to your programs so that they can be used in a cleaner way, or at least that's the theory.

I am now going to try to teach you the beginnings of object-oriented programming, classes, and objects using what you already know about dictionaries and modules. My problem though is that object-oriented programming (a.k.a. OOP) is just plain weird. You have to simply struggle with this, try to understand what I say here, type in the code, and then in the next exercise I'll hammer it in.

Here we go.

Modules Are Like Dictionaries

You know how a dictionary is created and used and that it is a way to map one thing to another. That means if you have a dictionary with a key 'apple' and you want to get it, then you do this:

```
mystuff = {'apple': "I AM APPLES!"}
print mystuff['apple']
```

Keep this idea of "get X from Y" in your head, and now think about modules. You've made a few so far and used them, in accordance with the following process:

1. You know that a module is a Python file with some functions or variables in it.

2. You then import that file.

3. And then you can access the functions or variables in that module with the '.' (dot) operator.

Imagine if I have a module that I decide to name mystuff.py, and I put a function in it called apple. Here's the module mystuff.py:

```
# this goes in mystuff.py
def apple():
    print "I AM APPLES!"
```

Once I have that, I can use that module with import and then access the apple function:

```
import mystuff
```

```
mystuff.apple()
```

I could also put a variable in it named `tangerine`, like this:

```
def apple():
    print "I AM APPLES!"

# this is just a variable
tangerine = "Living reflection of a dream"
```

Then again I can access that the same way:

```
import mystuff

mystuff.apple()
print mystuff.tangerine
```

Refer back to the dictionary, and you should start to see how this is similar to using a dictionary, but the syntax is different. Let's compare:

```
mystuff['apple'] # get apple from dict
mystuff.apple() # get apple from the module
mystuff.tangerine # same thing, it's just a variable
```

This means we have a *very* common pattern in Python:

1.   Take a key=value style container.

2.   Get something out of it by the key's name.

In the case of the dictionary, the key is a string and the syntax is [key]. In the case of the module, the key is an identifier, and the syntax is .key. Other than that, they are nearly the same thing.

Classes Are Like Modules

A way to think about a module is that it is a specialized dictionary that can store Python code so you can get to it with the '.' operator. Python also has another construct that serves a similar purpose called a `class`. A `class` is a way to take a grouping of functions and data and place them inside a container so you can access them with the '.' (dot) operator.

If I were to create a class just like the `mystuff` module, I'd do something like this:

```
class MyStuff(object):

    def __init__(self):
```

```
        self.tangerine = "And now a thousand years between"

def apple(self):
    print "I AM CLASSY APPLES!"
```

That looks complicated compared to modules, and there is definitely a lot going on by comparison, but you should be able to make out how this is like a "mini-module" with MyStuff having an apple() function in it. What is probably confusing with this is the __init__() function and use of self.tangerine for setting the tangerine variable.

Here's why classes are used instead of modules: You can take the above class and use it to craft many of them, millions at a time if you want, and they won't interfere with each other. With modules, when you import there is only one for the entire program, unless you do some monster hacks.

Before you can understand this though, you need to know what an "object" is and how to work with MyStuff just like you do with the mystuff.py module.

Objects Are Like Mini-Imports

If a class is like a "mini-module," then there has to be a similar concept to import but for classes. That concept is called "instantiate," which is just a fancy, obnoxious, overly smart way to say "create." When you instantiate a class, what you get is called an object.

The way you do this is you call the class like it's a function, like this:

```
thing = MyStuff()
thing.apple()
print thing.tangerine
```

The first line is the "instantiate" operation, and it's a lot like calling a function. However, when you call this, there's a sequence of events that Python coordinates for you. I'll go through them using the above code for MyStuff:

1. Python looks for MyStuff() and sees that it is a class you've defined.

2. Python crafts an empty object with all the functions you've specified in the class using def.

3. Python then looks to see if you made a "magic" __init__ function, and if you have, it calls that function to initialize your newly created empty object.

4. In the MyStuff function __init__ I then get this extra variable self, which is that empty object Python made for me, and I can set variables on it just like you would with a module, dict, or other object.

5. In this case, I set self.tangerine to a song lyric and then I've initialized this object.

6. Now Python can take this newly minted object and assign it to the thing variable for me to work with.

That's the basics of how Python does this "mini-import" when you call a class like a function. Remember that this is *not* giving you the class, but instead it is using the class as a *blueprint* for how to build a copy of that type of thing.

Keep in mind that I'm giving you a slightly inaccurate idea for how these work so that you can start to build up an understanding of classes based on what you know of modules. The truth is, classes and objects suddenly diverge from modules at this point. If I were being totally honest, I'd say something more like this:

- Classes are like blueprints or definitions for creating new mini-modules.

- Instantiation is how you make one of these mini-modules *and* import it at the same time.

- The resulting created mini-module is called an object and you then assign it to a variable to work with it.

After this, though, classes and objects become very different from modules, and this should only serve as a way for you to bridge over to understanding classes.

Getting Things from Things

I now have three ways to get things from things:

```
# dict style
mystuff['apples']

# module style
mystuff.apples()
print mystuff.tangerine

# class style
thing = MyStuff()
thing.apples()
print thing.tangerine
```

A First-Class Example

You should start seeing the similarities in these three key=value container types and probably have a bunch of questions. Hang on with the questions, as the next exercise is going to hammer home your "object-oriented vocabulary." In this exercise, I just want you to type in this code and get it working so that you have some experience before moving on.

ex40.py

```
1    class Song(object):
2
3        def __init__(self, lyrics):
```

```
4               self.lyrics = lyrics
5
6        def sing_me_a_song(self):
7            for line in self.lyrics:
8                print line
9
10   happy_bday = Song(["Happy birthday to you",
11                       "I don't want to get sued",
12                       "So I'll stop right there"])
13
14   bulls_on_parade = Song(["They rally around the family",
15                       "With pockets full of shells"])
16
17   happy_bday.sing_me_a_song()
18
19   bulls_on_parade.sing_me_a_song()
```

What You Should See

```
$ python ex40.py
Happy birthday to you
I don't want to get sued
So I'll stop right there
They rally around the family
With pockets full of shells
```

Study Drills

1. Write some more songs using this, and make sure you understand that you're passing a list of strings as the lyrics.

2. Put the lyrics in a separate variable, then pass that variable to the class to use instead.

3. See if you can hack on this and make it do more things. Don't worry if you have no idea how, just give it a try, see what happens. Break it, trash it, thrash it, you can't hurt it.

4. Search online for "object-oriented programming" and try to overflow your brain with what you read. Don't worry if it makes absolutely no sense to you. Half of that stuff makes no sense to me either.

Common Student Questions

Why do I need self when I make __init__ or other functions for classes?
If you don't have self, then code like cheese = 'Frank' is ambiguous. That code isn't clear about whether you mean the *instance's* cheese attribute *or* a local variable named cheese. With self.cheese = 'Frank' it's very clear you mean the instance attribute self.cheese.

Learning to Speak Object Oriented

In this exercise, I'm going to teach you how to speak "object oriented." What I'll do is give you a small set of words with definitions you need to know. Then I'll give you a set of sentences with holes in them that you'll have to understand. Finally, I'm going to give you a large set of exercises that you have to complete to make these sentences solid in your vocabulary.

Word Drills

- class—Tell Python to make a new kind of thing.

- object—Two meanings: the most basic kind of thing, and any instance of some thing.

- instance—What you get when you tell Python to create a class.

- def—How you define a function inside a class.

- self—Inside the functions in a class, self is a variable for the instance/object being accessed.

- inheritance—The concept that one class can inherit traits from another class, much like you and your parents.

- composition—The concept that a class can be composed of other classes as parts, much like how a car has wheels.

- attribute—A property classes have that are from composition and are usually variables.

- is-a—A phrase to say that something inherits from another, as in a "salmon" is-a "fish."

- has-a—A phrase to say that something is composed of other things or has a trait, as in "a salmon has-a mouth."

Take some time to make flash cards for those and memorize them. As usual this won't make too much sense until after you're done with this exercise, but you need to know the base words first.

Phrase Drills

Next I have a list of Python code snippets on the left and the English sentences for them:

class X(Y) "Make a class named X that is-a Y."

class X(object): def __init__(self, J) "class X has-a __init__ that takes self and J parameters."

class X(object): def M(self, J)   "class X has-a function named M that takes self and J parameters."

foo = X()   "Set foo to an instance of class X."

foo.M(J)   "From foo get the M function, and call it with parameters self, J."

foo.K = Q   "From foo get the K attribute, and set it to Q."

In each of these where you see X, Y, M, J, K, Q, and foo, you can treat those like blank spots. For example, I can also write these sentences as follows:

1. "Make a class named ??? that is-a Y."

2. "class ??? has-a __init__ that takes self and ??? parameters."

3. "class ??? has-a function named ??? that takes self and ??? parameters."

4. "Set foo to an instance of class ???."

5. "From foo get the ??? function, and call it with self=??? and parameters ???."

6. "From foo get the ??? attribute and set it to ???."

Again, write these on some flash cards and drill them. Put the Python code snippet on the front and the sentence on the back. You *have* to be able to say the sentence exactly the same every time whenever you see that form. Not sort of the same, but exactly the same.

Combined Drills

The final preparation for you is to combine the words drills with the phrase drills. What I want you to do for this drill is this:

1. Take a phrase card and drill it.

2. Flip it over and read the sentence, and for each word in the sentence that is in your words drills, get that card.

3. Drill those words for that sentence.

4. Keep going until you are bored, then take a break and do it again.

A Reading Test

I now have a little Python hack that will drill you on these words you know in an infinite manner. This is a simple script you should be able to figure out, and the only thing it does is use a library called `urllib` to download a list of words I have. Here's the script, which you should enter into `oop_test.py` to work with it:

ex41.py

```
1    import random
2    from urllib import urlopen
3    import sys
4
5    WORD_URL = "http://learncodethehardway.org/words.txt"
6    WORDS = []
7
8    PHRASES = {
9        "class %%%(%%%):":
10           "Make a class named %%% that is-a %%%.",
11       "class %%%(object):\n\tdef __init__(self, ***)" :
12           "class %%% has-a __init__ that takes self and *** parameters.",
13       "class %%%(object):\n\tdef ***(self, @@@)":
14           "class %%% has-a function named *** that takes self and @@@ parameters.",
15       "*** = %%%()":
16           "Set *** to an instance of class %%%.",
17       "***.***(@@@)":
18           "From *** get the *** function, and call it with parameters self, @@@.",
19       "***.*** = '***'":
20           "From *** get the *** attribute and set it to '***'."
21   }
22
23   # do they want to drill phrases first
24   PHRASE_FIRST = False
25   if len(sys.argv) == 2 and sys.argv[1] == "english":
26       PHRASE_FIRST = True
27
28   # load up the words from the website
29   for word in urlopen(WORD_URL).readlines():
30       WORDS.append(word.strip())
31
32
33   def convert(snippet, phrase):
34       class_names = [w.capitalize() for w in
35                       random.sample(WORDS, snippet.count("%%%"))]
36       other_names = random.sample(WORDS, snippet.count("***"))
37       results = []
38       param_names = []
39
40       for i in range(0, snippet.count("@@@")):
41           param_count = random.randint(1,3)
42           param_names.append(', '.join(random.sample(WORDS, param_count)))
43
44       for sentence in snippet, phrase:
45           result = sentence[:]
46
47           # fake class names
```

```
48              for word in class_names:
49                  result = result.replace("%%%", word, 1)
50
51              # fake other names
52              for word in other_names:
53                  result = result.replace("***", word, 1)
54
55              # fake parameter lists
56              for word in param_names:
57                  result = result.replace("@@@", word, 1)
58
59              results.append(result)
60
61      return results
62
63
64  # keep going until they hit CTRL-D
65  try:
66      while True:
67          snippets = PHRASES.keys()
68          random.shuffle(snippets)
69
70          for snippet in snippets:
71              phrase = PHRASES[snippet]
72              question, answer = convert(snippet, phrase)
73              if PHRASE_FIRST:
74                  question, answer = answer, question
75
76              print question
77
78              raw_input("> ")
79              print "ANSWER:  %s\n\n" % answer
80  except EOFError:
81      print "\nBye"
```

Run this script and try to translate the "object-oriented phrases" into English translations. You should see that the PHRASES dict has both forms and you just have to enter the correct one.

Practice English to Code

Next you should run the script with the "english" option so that you drill the inverse operation.

Remember that these phrases are using nonsense words. Part of learning to read code well is to stop placing so much meaning on the names used for variables and classes. Too often people will read a word like "Cork" and suddenly get derailed because that word will confuse them about the meaning. In the above example, "Cork" is just an arbitrary name chosen for a class. Don't put any other meaning into it, and instead treat it like the patterns I've given you.

Reading More Code

You are now to go on a new quest to read even more code and, this time, to read the phrases you just learned in the code you read. You will look for all the files with classes, and then do the following:

1.   For each class, give its name and what other classes it inherits from.

2.   Under that, list every function it has and the parameters they take.

3.   List all the attributes it uses on self.

4.   For each attribute, give the class it is.

The goal is to go through real code and start learning to "pattern match" the phrases you just learned against how they're used. If you drill this enough, you should start to see these patterns shout at you in the code, whereas before they just seemed like vague blank spots you didn't know.

Common Student Questions

What does `result = sentence[:]` do?
That's a Python way of copying a list. You're using the list slice syntax `[:]` to effectively make a slice from the very first element to the very last one.

This script is hard to get running!
By this point, you should be able to type this in and get it working. It does have a few little tricks here and there, but there's nothing complex about it. Just do all the things you've learned so far to debug scripts like this.

Is-A, Has-A, Objects, and Classes

An important concept that you have to understand is the difference between a class and an object. The problem is, there is no real "difference" between a class and an object. They are actually the same thing at different points in time. I will demonstrate by a Zen koan:

What is the difference between a Fish and a Salmon?

Did that question sort of confuse you? Really sit down and think about it for a minute. I mean, a Fish and a Salmon are different but, wait, they are the same thing, right? A Salmon is a *kind* of Fish, so I mean it's not different. But at the same time, because a Salmon is a particular *type* of Fish, it's actually different from all other Fish. That's what makes it a Salmon and not a Halibut. So a Salmon and a Fish are the same but different. Weird.

This question is confusing because most people do not think about real things this way, but they intuitively understand them. You do not need to think about the difference between a Fish and a Salmon because you *know* how they are related. You know a Salmon is a *kind* of Fish and that there are other kinds of Fish without having to understand that.

Let's take it one step further: say you have a bucket full of three Salmon and, because you are a nice person, you have decided to name them Frank, Joe, and Mary. Now, think about this question:

What is the difference between Mary and a Salmon?

Again, this is a weird question, but it's a bit easier than the Fish versus Salmon question. You know that Mary is a Salmon, and so she's not really different. She's just a specific "instance" of a Salmon. Joe and Frank are also instances of Salmon. What do I mean when I say "instance"? I mean they were created from some other Salmon and now represent a real thing that has Salmon-like attributes.

Now for the mind-bending idea: Fish is a class, and Salmon is a class, and Mary is an object. Think about that for a second. Alright let's break it down real slow and see if you get it.

A Fish is a class, meaning it's not a *real* thing, but rather a word we attach to instances of things with similar attributes. Got fins? Got gills? Lives in water? Alright it's probably a Fish.

Someone with a PhD then comes along and says, "No, my young friend, *this* Fish is actually *Salmo salar*, affectionately known as a Salmon." This professor has just clarified the Fish further and made a new class called "Salmon" that has more specific attributes. Longer nose, reddish flesh, big, lives in the ocean or fresh water, tasty? OK, probably a Salmon.

Finally, a cook comes along and tells the PhD, "No, you see this Salmon right here, I'll call her Mary and I'm going to make a tasty fillet out of her with a nice sauce." Now you have this *instance* of a Salmon (which also is an instance of a Fish) named Mary turned into something real that is filling your belly. It has become an object.

There you have it: Mary is a kind of Salmon that is a kind of Fish. object is a class is a class.

How This Looks in Code

This is a weird concept, but to be very honest, you only have to worry about it when you make new classes and when you use a class. I will show you two tricks to help you figure out whether something is a class or object.

First, you need to learn two catch phrases: "is-a" and "has-a." You use the phrase is-a when you talk about objects and classes being related to each other by a class relationship. You use has-a when you talk about objects and classes that are related only because they *reference* each other.

Now, go through this piece of code and replace each ## ?? comment with a replacement comment that says whether the next line represents an is-a or a has-a relationship and what that relationship is. In the beginning of the code, I've laid out a few examples, so you just have to write the remaining ones.

Remember, is-a is the relationship between Fish and Salmon, while has-a is the relationship between Salmon and Gills.

ex42.py

```
1    ## Animal is-a object (yes, sort of confusing) look at the extra credit
2    class Animal(object):
3        pass
4
5    ## ??
6    class Dog(Animal):
7
8        def __init__(self, name):
9            ## ??
10           self.name = name
11
12   ## ??
13   class Cat(Animal):
14
15       def __init__(self, name):
16           ## ??
17           self.name = name
18
19   ## ??
20   class Person(object):
```

```
21
22      def __init__(self, name):
23          ## ??
24          self.name = name
25
26          ## Person has-a pet of some kind
27          self.pet = None
28
29  ## ??
30  class Employee(Person):
31
32      def __init__(self, name, salary):
33          ## ?? hmm what is this strange magic?
34          super(Employee, self).__init__(name)
35          ## ??
36          self.salary = salary
37
38  ## ??
39  class Fish(object):
40      pass
41
42  ## ??
43  class Salmon(Fish):
44      pass
45
46  ## ??
47  class Halibut(Fish):
48      pass
49
50
51  ## rover is-a Dog
52  rover = Dog("Rover")
53
54  ## ??
55  satan = Cat("Satan")
56
57  ## ??
58  mary = Person("Mary")
59
60  ## ??
61  mary.pet = satan
62
63  ## ??
64  frank = Employee("Frank", 120000)
65
66  ## ??
67  frank.pet = rover
68
69  ## ??
70  flipper = Fish()
71
```

```
72   ## ??
73   crouse = Salmon()
74
75   ## ??
76   harry = Halibut()
```

About class Name(object)

Remember how I was yelling at you to always use class Name(object) and I couldn't tell you why? Now I can tell you, because you just learned about the difference between a class and an object. I couldn't tell you until now because you would have just been confused and couldn't learn to use the technology.

What happened is Python's original rendition of class was broken in many serious ways. By the time they admitted the fault, it was too late, and they had to support it. In order to fix the problem, they needed some "new class" style so that the "old classes" would keep working but you could use the new, more correct version.

This is where "class is-a object" comes in. They decided that they would use the word "object," lowercased, to be the "class" that you inherit from to make a class. Confusing, right? A class inherits from the class named object to make a class, but it's not an object. (Really it's a class, but do not forget to inherit from object.)

Exactly. The choice of one single word meant that I couldn't teach you about this until now. Now you can try to understand the concept of a class that is an object, if you like.

However, I would suggest you do not. Just completely ignore the idea of old style versus new style classes and assume that Python always requires (object) when you make a class. Save your brain power for something important.

Study Drills

1. Research why Python added this strange object class and what that means.

2. Is it possible to use a class like it's an object?

3. Fill out the animals, fish, and people in this exercise with functions that make them do things. See what happens when functions are in a "base class" like Animal versus Dog.

4. Find other people's code and work out all the is-a and has-a relationships.

5. Make some new relationships that are lists and dicts so you can also have "has-many" relationships.

6.   Do you think there's a such thing as an "is-many" relationship? Read about "multiple inheritance," then avoid it if you can.

Common Student Questions

What are these ## ?? comments for?
Those are "fill-in-the-blank" comments that you are supposed to fill in with the right "is-a," "has-a" concepts. Re-read this exercise and look at the other comments to see what I mean.

What is the point of self.pet = None?
That makes sure that the self.pet attribute of that class is set to a default of None.

What does super(Employee, self).__init__(name) do?
That's how you can run the __init__ method of a parent class reliably. Go search for "python super" and read the various advice on it being evil and good for you.

Basic Object-Oriented Analysis and Design

I'm going to describe a process to use when you want to build something using Python, specifically with object-oriented programming (OOP). What I mean by a "process" is that I'll give you a set of steps that you do in order but that you aren't meant to be a slave to or that will totally always work for every problem. They are just a good starting point for many programming problems and shouldn't be considered the *only* way to solve these types of problems. This process is just one way to do it that you can follow.

The process is as follows:

1. Write or draw about the problem.

2. Extract key concepts from #1 and research them.

3. Create a class hierarchy and object map for the concepts.

4. Code the classes and a test to run them.

5. Repeat and refine.

The way to look at this process is that it is "top down," meaning it starts from the very abstract, loose idea and then slowly refines it until the idea is solid and something you can code.

First I start by just writing about the problem and trying to think up anything I can about it. Maybe I'll even draw a diagram or two, maybe a map of some kind, or even write myself a series of emails describing the problem. This gives me a way to express the key concepts in the problem and also explore what I might already know about it.

Then I go through these notes, drawings, and descriptions, and I pull out the key concepts. There's a simple trick to doing this: Simply make a list of all the *nouns* and *verbs* in your writing and drawings, then write out how they're related. This gives me a good list of names for classes, objects, and functions in the next step. I take this list of concepts and then research any that I don't understand so I can refine them further if I needed.

Once I have my list of concepts, I create a simple outline/tree of the concepts and how they are related as classes. You can usually take your list of nouns and start asking, "Is this one like other concept nouns? That means they have a common parent class, so what is it called?" Keep doing this until you have a class hierarchy that's just a simple tree list or a diagram. Then take the *verbs* you have and see if those are function names for each class and put them in your tree.

With this class hierarchy figured out, I sit down and write some basic skeleton code that has just the classes, their functions, and nothing more. I then write a test that runs this code and makes sure the classes I've made make sense and work right. Sometimes I may write the test first though, and other times I might write a little test, a little code, a little test, and so on, until I have the whole thing built.

Finally, I keep cycling over this process, repeating it and refining as I go and making it as clear as I can before doing more implementation. If I get stuck at any particular part because of a concept or problem I haven't anticipated, then I sit down and start the process over on just that part to figure it out more before continuing.

I will now go through this process while coming up with a game engine and a game for this exercise.

The Analysis of a Simple Game Engine

The game I want to make is called "Gothons from Planet Percal #25" and will be a small space adventure game. With nothing more than that concept in my mind, I can explore the idea and figure out how to make the game come to life.

Write or Draw about the Problem

I'm going to write a little paragraph for the game:

"Aliens have invaded a space ship and our hero has to go through a maze of rooms defeating them so he can escape into an escape pod to the planet below. The game will be more like a Zork or Adventure type game with text outputs and funny ways to die. The game will involve an engine that runs a map full of rooms or scenes. Each room will print its own description when the player enters it and then tell the engine what room to run next out of the map."

At this point, I have a good idea for the game and how it would run, so now I want to describe each scene:

> **Death**   This is when the player dies and should be something funny.
>
> **Central Corridor**   This is the starting point and has a Gothon already standing there, which the player has to defeat with a joke before continuing.
>
> **Laser Weapon Armory**   This is where the hero gets a neutron bomb to blow up the ship before getting to the escape pod. It has a keypad he has to guess the number for.
>
> **The Bridge**   Another battle scene with a Gothon where the hero places the bomb.
>
> **Escape Pod**   Where the hero escapes but only after guessing the right escape pod.

At this point, I might draw out a map of these, maybe write more descriptions of each room—whatever comes to mind as I explore the problem.

Extract Key Concepts and Research Them

I now have enough information to extract some of the nouns out and analyze their class hierarchy. First I make a list of all the nouns:

- Alien
- Player
- Ship
- Maze
- Room
- Scene
- Gothon
- Escape Pod
- Planet
- Map
- Engine
- Death
- Central Corridor
- Laser Weapon Armory
- The Bridge

I would also possibly go through all the verbs and see if they are anything that might be good function names, but I'll skip that for now.

At this point, you might also research each of these concepts and anything you don't know right now. For example, I might play a few of these types of games and make sure I know how they work. I might go research how ships are designed or how bombs work. Maybe I'll go research some technical issue like how to store the game's state in a database. After I've done this research, I might start over at step #1 based on new information I have and rewrite my description and extract new concepts.

Create a Class Hierarchy and Object Map for the Concepts

Once I have that, I turn it into a class hierarchy by asking, "What is similar to other things?" I also ask, "What is basically just another word for another thing?"

Right away I see that I can say "Room" and "Scene" are basically the same thing, depending on how I want to do things. I'm going to pick "Scene" for this game. Then I see that all the specific rooms like "Central Corridor" are basically just Scenes. I see also that Death is basically a Scene, which confirms my choice of "Scene" over "Room," since you can have a death scene, but a death room is kind of odd. "Maze" and "Map" are basically the same, so I'm going to go with "Map" since I used it more often. I don't want to do a battle system, so I'm going to ignore "Alien" and "Player" and save that for later. And the "Planet" could also just be another scene instead of something specific.

After that thought process, I start to make a class hierarchy that looks like this in my text editor:

```
* Map
* Engine
* Scene
  * Death
  * Central Corridor
  * Laser Weapon Armory
  * The Bridge
  * Escape Pod
```

I would also then go through and figure out what actions are needed on each thing based on verbs in the description. For example, I know that from the above description I'm going to need a way to "run" the engine, "get the next scene" from the map, get the "opening scene," and "enter" a scene. I'll add those like this:

```
* Map
  - next_scene
  - opening_scene
* Engine
  - play
* Scene
  - enter
  * Death
  * Central Corridor
  * Laser Weapon Armory
  * The Bridge
  * Escape Pod
```

Notice how I just put -enter under Scene since I know that all the scenes under it will inherit it and have to override it later.

Code the Classes and a Test to Run Them

Once I have this tree of classes and some of the functions, I open up a source file in my editor and try to write the code for it. Usually I'll just copy-paste the above tree into the source file and then edit it into classes. Here's a small example of how this might look at first, with a simple little test at the end of the file.

ex43_classes.py

```
1    class Scene(object):
2
3        def enter(self):
4            pass
5
6
7    class Engine(object):
8
9        def __init__(self, scene_map):
10           pass
11
12       def play(self):
13           pass
14
15   class Death(Scene):
16
17       def enter(self):
18           pass
19
20   class CentralCorridor(Scene):
21
22       def enter(self):
23           pass
24
25   class LaserWeaponArmory(Scene):
26
27       def enter(self):
28           pass
29
30   class TheBridge(Scene):
31
32       def enter(self):
33           pass
34
35   class EscapePod(Scene):
36
37       def enter(self):
38           pass
39
40
41   class Map(object):
42
43       def __init__(self, start_scene):
44           pass
45
46       def next_scene(self, scene_name):
47           pass
48
```

```
49        def opening_scene(self):
50            pass
51
52
53    a_map = Map('central_corridor')
54    a_game = Engine(a_map)
55    a_game.play()
```

In this file, you can see that I simply replicated the hierarchy I wanted and then a little bit of code at the end to run it and see if it all works in this basic structure. In the later sections of this exercise, you'll fill in the rest of this code and make it work to match the description of the game.

Repeat and Refine

The last step in my little process isn't so much a step as it is a `while-loop`. You don't ever do this as a one-pass operation. Instead, you go back over the whole process again and refine it based on information you've learned from later steps. Sometimes I'll get to step #3 and realize that I need to work on #1 and #2 more, so I'll stop and go back and work on those. Sometimes I'll get a flash of inspiration and jump to the end to code up the solution in my head while I have it there, but then I'll go back and do the previous steps to make sure I cover all the possibilities I have.

The other idea in this process is that it's not just something you do at one single level but something that you can do at every level when you run into a particular problem. Let's say I don't know how to write the `Engine.play` method yet. I can stop and do this whole process on *just* that one function to figure out how to write it.

Top Down vs. Bottom Up

The process I just described is typically labeled "top down" since it starts at the most abstract concepts (the top) and works its way down to actual implementation. I want you to use this process I just described when analyzing problems in the book from now on, but you should know that there's another way to solve problems in programming that starts with code and goes "up" to the abstract concepts. This other way is labeled "bottom up." Here are the general steps you follow to do this:

1. Take a small piece of the problem; hack on some code and get it to run barely.

2. Refine the code into something more formal with classes and automated tests.

3. Extract the key concepts you're using and try to find research for them.

4. Write up a description of what's really going on.

5. Go back and refine the code, possibly throwing it out and starting over.

6. Repeat, moving on to some other piece of the problem.

This process I find is better once you're more solid at programming and are naturally thinking in code about problems. This process is very good when you know small pieces of the overall puzzle but maybe don't have enough information yet about the overall concept. Breaking it down in little pieces and exploring with code then helps you slowly grind away at the problem until you've solved it. However, remember that your solution will probably be meandering and weird, so that's why my version of this process involves going back and finding research then cleaning things up based on what you've learned.

The Code for "Gothons from Planet Percal #25"

Stop! I'm going to show you my final solution to the above problem but I don't want you to just jump in and type this up. I want *you* to take the rough skeleton code I did above and then try to make it work based on the description. Once you have your solution, then you can come back and see how I did it.

I'm going to break this final file ex43.py down into sections and explain each one rather than dump all the code at once.

ex43.py

```
1    from sys import exit
2    from random import randint
```

This is just our basic imports for the game, nothing fancy really.

ex43.py

```
1    class Scene(object):
2
3        def enter(self):
4            print "This scene is not yet configured. Subclass it and implement enter()."
5            exit(1)
```

As you saw in the skeleton code, I have a base class for Scene that will have the common things that all scenes do. In this simple program, they don't do much, so this is more a demonstration of what you would do to make a base class.

ex43.py

```
1    class Engine(object):
2
3        def __init__(self, scene_map):
4            self.scene_map = scene_map
5
6        def play(self):
7            current_scene = self.scene_map.opening_scene()
8
9            while True:
```

```
10                    print "\n--------"
11                    next_scene_name = current_scene.enter()
12                    current_scene = self.scene_map.next_scene(next_scene_name)
```

I also have my Engine class and you can see how I'm already just using the methods for Map. opening_scene and Map.next_scene. Because I've done a bit of planning, I can just assume I'll write those and then use them before I've written the Map class.

ex43.py

```
1    class Death(Scene):
2
3        quips = [
4            "You died.  You kinda suck at this.",
5            "Your mom would be proud...if she were smarter.",
6            "Such a luser.",
7            "I have a small puppy that's better at this."
8        ]
9
10       def enter(self):
11           print Death.quips[randint(0, len(self.quips)-1)]
12           exit(1)
```

My first scene is the odd scene named Death, which shows you the simplest kind of scene you can write.

ex43.py

```
1    class CentralCorridor(Scene):
2
3      def enter(self):
4        print "The Gothons of Planet Percal #25 have invaded your ship and destroyed"
5        print "your entire crew.  You are the last surviving member and your last"
6        print "mission is to get the neutron destruct bomb from the Weapons Armory,"
7        print "put it in the bridge, and blow the ship up after getting into an "
8        print "escape pod."
9        print "\n"
10       print "You're running down the central corridor to the Weapons Armory when"
11       print "a Gothon jumps out, red scaly skin, dark grimy teeth, and evil clown costume"
12       print "flowing around his hate filled body.  He's blocking the door to the"
13       print "Armory and about to pull a weapon to blast you."
14
15       action = raw_input("> ")
16
17       if action == "shoot!":
18         print "Quick on the draw you yank out your blaster and fire it at the Gothon."
19         print "His clown costume is flowing and moving around his body, which throws"
20         print "off your aim. Your laser hits his costume but misses him entirely. This"
21         print "completely ruins his brand new costume his mother bought him, which"
22         print "makes him fly into a rage and blast you repeatedly in the face until"
23         print "you are dead.  Then he eats you."
24         return 'death'
```

```
25
26       elif action == "dodge!":
27         print "Like a world class boxer you dodge, weave, slip and slide right"
28         print "as the Gothon's blaster cranks a laser past your head."
29         print "In the middle of your artful dodge your foot slips and you"
30         print "bang your head on the metal wall and pass out."
31         print "You wake up shortly after only to die as the Gothon stomps on"
32         print "your head and eats you."
33         return 'death'
34
35       elif action == "tell a joke":
36         print "Lucky for you they made you learn Gothon insults in the academy."
37         print "You tell the one Gothon joke you know:"
38         print "Lbhe zbgure vf fb sng, jura fur fvgf nebhaq gur ubhfr, fur fvgf nebhaq gur ubhfr."
39         print "The Gothon stops, tries not to laugh, then busts out laughing and can't move."
40         print "While he's laughing you run up and shoot him square in the head"
41         print "putting him down, then jump through the Weapon Armory door."
42         return 'laser_weapon_armory'
43
44       else:
45         print "DOES NOT COMPUTE!"
46         return 'central_corridor'
```

After that, I've created the `CentralCorridor`, which is the start of the game. I'm doing the scenes for the game before the Map because I need to reference them later.

ex43.py

```
1     class LaserWeaponArmory(Scene):
2
3        def enter(self):
4            print "You do a dive roll into the Weapon Armory, crouch and scan the room"
5            print "for more Gothons that might be hiding.  It's dead quiet, too quiet."
6            print "You stand up and run to the far side of the room and find the"
7            print "neutron bomb in its container.  There's a keypad lock on the box"
8            print "and you need the code to get the bomb out.  If you get the code"
9            print "wrong 10 times then the lock closes forever and you can't"
10           print "get the bomb.  The code is 3 digits."
11           code = "%d%d%d" % (randint(1,9), randint(1,9), randint(1,9))
12           guess = raw_input("[keypad]> ")
13           guesses = 0
14
15           while guess != code and guesses < 10:
16             print "BZZZZEDDD!"
17             guesses += 1
18             guess = raw_input("[keypad]> ")
19
20           if guess == code:
21             print "The container clicks open and the seal breaks, letting gas out."
22             print "You grab the neutron bomb and run as fast as you can to the"
23             print "bridge where you must place it in the right spot."
```

```
24                  return 'the_bridge'
25              else:
26                  print "The lock buzzes one last time and then you hear a sickening"
27                  print "melting sound as the mechanism is fused together."
28                  print "You decide to sit there, and finally the Gothons blow up the"
29                  print "ship from their ship and you die."
30                  return 'death'
31
32
33
34      class TheBridge(Scene):
35
36          def enter(self):
37              print "You burst onto the Bridge with the neutron destruct bomb"
38              print "under your arm and surprise 5 Gothons who are trying to"
39              print "take control of the ship.  Each of them has an even uglier"
40              print "clown costume than the last.  They haven't pulled their"
41              print "weapons out yet, as they see the active bomb under your"
42              print "arm and don't want to set it off."
43
44              action = raw_input("> ")
45
46              if action == "throw the bomb":
47                  print "In a panic you throw the bomb at the group of Gothons"
48                  print "and make a leap for the door.  Right as you drop it a"
49                  print "Gothon shoots you right in the back killing you."
50                  print "As you die you see another Gothon frantically try to disarm"
51                  print "the bomb. You die knowing they will probably blow up when"
52                  print "it goes off."
53                  return 'death'
54
55              elif action == "slowly place the bomb":
56                  print "You point your blaster at the bomb under your arm"
57                  print "and the Gothons put their hands up and start to sweat."
58                  print "You inch backward to the door, open it, and then carefully"
59                  print "place the bomb on the floor, pointing your blaster at it."
60                  print "You then jump back through the door, punch the close button"
61                  print "and blast the lock so the Gothons can't get out."
62                  print "Now that the bomb is placed you run to the escape pod to"
63                  print "get off this tin can."
64                  return 'escape_pod'
65              else:
66                  print "DOES NOT COMPUTE!"
67                  return "the_bridge"
68
69
70      class EscapePod(Scene):
71
72          def enter(self):
73              print "You rush through the ship desperately trying to make it to"
74              print "the escape pod before the whole ship explodes.  It seems like"
```

```
75              print "hardly any Gothons are on the ship, so your run is clear of"
76              print "interference.  You get to the chamber with the escape pods, and"
77              print "now need to pick one to take.  Some of them could be damaged"
78              print "but you don't have time to look.  There's 5 pods, which one"
79              print "do you take?"
80
81              good_pod = randint(1,5)
82              guess = raw_input("[pod #]> ")
83
84
85              if int(guess) != good_pod:
86                  print "You jump into pod %s and hit the eject button." % guess
87                  print "The pod escapes out into the void of space, then"
88                  print "implodes as the hull ruptures, crushing your body"
89                  print "into jam jelly."
90                  return 'death'
91              else:
92                  print "You jump into pod %s and hit the eject button." % guess
93                  print "The pod easily slides out into space heading to"
94                  print "the planet below.  As it flies to the planet, you look"
95                  print "back and see your ship implode then explode like a"
96                  print "bright star, taking out the Gothon ship at the same"
97                  print "time.  You won!"
98
99
100             return 'finished'
```

This is the rest of the game's scenes, and since I know I need them and have thought about how they'll flow together, I'm able to code them up directly.

Incidentally, I wouldn't just type all this code in. Remember I said to try to build this incrementally, one little bit at a time. I'm just showing you the final result.

ex43.py

```
1    class Map(object):
2
3        scenes = {
4            'central_corridor': CentralCorridor(),
5            'laser_weapon_armory': LaserWeaponArmory(),
6            'the_bridge': TheBridge(),
7            'escape_pod': EscapePod(),
8            'death': Death()
9        }
10
11       def __init__(self, start_scene):
12           self.start_scene = start_scene
13
14       def next_scene(self, scene_name):
15           return Map.scenes.get(scene_name)
16
17       def opening_scene(self):
18           return self.next_scene(self.start_scene)
```

After that, I have my Map class, and you can see it is storing each scene by name in a dictionary, and then I refer to that dict with Map.scenes. This is also why the map comes after the scenes—because the dictionary has to refer to them so they have to exist.

ex43.py

```
1    a_map = Map('central_corridor')
2    a_game = Engine(a_map)
3    a_game.play()
```

Finally I've got my code that runs the game by making a Map then handing that map to an Engine before calling play to make the game work.

What You Should See

Make sure you understand the game and that you tried to solve it yourself first. One thing to do if you're stumped is just go cheat a little bit. Take a look real quick in the book, then get your "Aha!" realization from my code, and go back to working on yours. Just try as hard as you can to solve it yourself first.

When I run my game it looks like this:

Exercise 43 Session

```
$ python ex43.py

--------

The Gothons of Planet Percal #25 have invaded your ship and destroyed
your entire crew.  You are the last surviving member and your last
mission is to get the neutron destruct bomb from the Weapons Armory,
put it in the bridge, and blow the ship up after getting into an
escape pod.


You're running down the central corridor to the Weapons Armory when
a Gothon jumps out, red scaly skin, dark grimy teeth, and evil clown costume
flowing around his hate filled body.  He's blocking the door to the
Armory and about to pull a weapon to blast you.
>   dodge!
Like a world class boxer you dodge, weave, slip and slide right
as the Gothon's blaster cranks a laser past your head.
In the middle of your artful dodge your foot slips and you
bang your head on the metal wall and pass out.
You wake up shortly after only to die as the Gothon stomps on
your head and eats you.


--------

I have a small puppy that's better at this.
```

Study Drills

1. I have a bug in this code. Why is the door lock guessing 11 times?

2. Explain how returning the next room works.

3. Add cheat codes to the game so you can get past the more difficult rooms. I can do this with two words on one line.

4. Go back to my description and analysis, then try to build a small combat system for the hero and the various Gothons he encounters.

5. This is actually a small version of something called a "finite state machine." Read about them. They might not make sense but try anyway.

Common Student Questions

Where can I find stories for my own games?
You can make them up, just like you would tell a story to a friend. Or you can also take simple scenes from a book or movie you like.

Inheritance vs. Composition

In the fairy tales about heroes defeating evil villains, there's always a dark forest of some kind. It could be a cave, a forest, another planet—just some place that everyone knows the hero shouldn't go. Of course, shortly after the villain is introduced, you find out, yes, the hero has to go to that stupid forest to kill the bad guy. It seems the hero just keeps getting into situations that require him to risk his life in this evil forest.

You rarely read fairy tales about the heroes who are smart enough to just avoid the whole situation entirely. You never hear a hero say, "Wait a minute, if I leave to make my fortunes on the high seas leaving Buttercup behind I could die and then she'd have to marry some ugly prince named Humperdink. Humperdink! I think I'll stay here and start a Farm Boy for Rent business." If he did that there'd be no fire swamp, dying, reanimation, sword fights, giants, or any kind of story really. Because of this, the forest in these stories seems to exist like a black hole that drags the hero in no matter what they do.

In object-oriented programming, *inheritance* is the evil forest. Experienced programmers know to avoid this evil because they know that deep inside the dark forest of inheritance is the evil queen, *multiple inheritance*. She likes to eat software and programmers with her massive complexity teeth, chewing on the flesh of the fallen. But the forest is so powerful and so tempting that nearly every programmer has to go into it and try to make it out alive with the evil queen's head before they can call themselves real programmers. You just can't resist the inheritance forest's pull, so you go in. After the adventure, you learn to just stay out of that stupid forest and bring an army if you are ever forced to go in again.

This is basically a funny way to say that I'm going to teach you something you should avoid, called *inheritance*. Programmers who are currently in the forest battling the queen will probably tell you that you have to go in. They say this because they need your help, since what they've created is probably too much for them to handle. But you should always remember this:

Most of the uses of inheritance can be simplified or replaced with composition, and multiple inheritance should be avoided at all costs.

What Is Inheritance?

Inheritance is used to indicate that one class will get most or all of its features from a parent class. This happens implicitly whenever you write `class Foo(Bar)`, which says "Make a class Foo that inherits from Bar." When you do this, the language makes any action that you do on instances of Foo also work as if they were done to an instance of Bar. Doing this lets you put common functionality in the Bar class, then specialize that functionality in the Foo class as needed.

When you are doing this kind of specialization, there are three ways that the parent and child classes can interact:

1. Actions on the child imply an action on the parent.

2. Actions on the child override the action on the parent.

3. Actions on the child alter the action on the parent.

I will now demonstrate each of these in order and show you code for them.

Implicit Inheritance

First I will show you the implicit actions that happen when you define a function in the parent, but *not* in the child.

ex44a.py

```
1    class Parent(object):
2
3        def implicit(self):
4            print "PARENT implicit()"
5
6    class Child(Parent):
7        pass
8
9    dad = Parent()
10   son = Child()
11
12   dad.implicit()
13   son.implicit()
```

The use of pass under the class Child: is how you tell Python that you want an empty block. This creates a class named Child but says that there's nothing new to define in it. Instead, it will inherit all its behavior from Parent. When you run this code you get the following:

Exercise 44a Session

```
$ python ex44a.py
PARENT implicit()
PARENT implicit()
```

Notice how even though I'm calling son.implicit() on line 16, and even though Child does *not* have an implicit function defined, it still works and it calls the one defined in Parent. This shows you that, if you put functions in a base class (i.e., Parent), then all subclasses (i.e., Child) will automatically get those features. Very handy for repetitive code you need in many classes.

Override Explicitly

The problem with implicitly having functions called is sometimes you want the child to behave differently. In this case, you want to override the function in the child, effectively replacing the functionality. To do this, just define a function with the same name in Child. Here's an example:

ex44b.py

```
1    class Parent(object):
2
3        def override(self):
4            print "PARENT override()"
5
6    class Child(Parent):
7
8        def override(self):
9            print "CHILD override()"
10
11    dad = Parent()
12    son = Child()
13
14    dad.override()
15    son.override()
```

In this example, I have a function named override in both classes, so let's see what happens when you run it.

Exercise 44b Session

```
$ python ex44b.py
PARENT override()
CHILD override()
```

As you can see, when line 14 runs, it runs the Parent.override function because that variable (dad) is a Parent. But when line 15 runs, it prints out the Child.override messages because son is an instance of Child and Child overrides that function by defining its own version.

Take a break right now and try playing with these two concepts before continuing.

Alter Before or After

The third way to use inheritance is a special case of overriding where you want to alter the behavior before or after the Parent class's version runs. You first override the function just like in the last example, but then you use a Python built-in function named super to get the Parent version to call. Here's the example of doing that so you can make sense of this description:

ex44c.py

```
1    class Parent(object):
2
```

```
3          def altered(self):
4              print "PARENT altered()"
5
6     class Child(Parent):
7
8          def altered(self):
9              print "CHILD, BEFORE PARENT altered()"
10             super(Child, self).altered()
11             print "CHILD, AFTER PARENT altered()"
12
13    dad = Parent()
14    son = Child()
15
16    dad.altered()
17    son.altered()
```

The important lines here are 9–11, where in the `Child` I do the following when `son.altered()` is called:

1. Because I've overridden `Parent.altered` the `Child.altered` version runs, and line 9 executes like you'd expect.

2. In this case, I want to do a before and after, so after line 9, I want to use `super` to get the `Parent.altered` version.

3. On line 10, I call `super(Child, self).altered()`, which is a lot like the `getattr` function you've used in the past, but it's aware of inheritance and will get the `Parent` class for you. You should be able to read this as "call super with arguments `Child` and `self`, then call the function `altered` on whatever it returns."

4. At this point, the `Parent.altered` version of the function runs, and that prints out the `Parent` message.

5. Finally, this returns from the `Parent.altered`, and the `Child.altered` function continues to print out the after message.

If you then run this, you should see the following:

Exercise 44c Session

```
$ python ex44c.py
PARENT altered()
CHILD, BEFORE PARENT altered()
PARENT altered()
CHILD, AFTER PARENT altered()
```

All Three Combined

To demonstrate all these, I have a final version that shows each kind of interaction from inheritance in one file:

ex44d.py

```
1    class Parent(object):
2
3        def override(self):
4            print "PARENT override()"
5
6        def implicit(self):
7            print "PARENT implicit()"
8
9        def altered(self):
10           print "PARENT altered()"
11
12   class Child(Parent):
13
14       def override(self):
15           print "CHILD override()"
16
17       def altered(self):
18           print "CHILD, BEFORE PARENT altered()"
19           super(Child, self).altered()
20           print "CHILD, AFTER PARENT altered()"
21
22   dad = Parent()
23   son = Child()
24
25   dad.implicit()
26   son.implicit()
27
28   dad.override()
29   son.override()
30
31   dad.altered()
32   son.altered()
```

Go through each line of this code, and write a comment explaining what that line does and whether it's an override or not. Then run it and see that you get what you expected:

Exercise 44d Session

```
$ python ex44d.py
PARENT implicit()
PARENT implicit()
PARENT override()
CHILD override()
PARENT altered()
CHILD, BEFORE PARENT altered()
```

```
PARENT altered()
CHILD, AFTER PARENT altered()
```

The Reason for super()

This should seem like common sense, but then we get into trouble with a thing called *multiple inheritance*. Multiple inheritance is when you define a class that inherits from one or *more* classes, like this:

```
class SuperFun(Child, BadStuff):
    pass
```

This is like saying, "Make a class named SuperFun that inherits from the classes Child and BadStuff at the same time."

In this case, whenever you have implicit actions on any SuperFun instance, Python has to look up the possible function in the class hierarchy for both Child and BadStuff, but it needs to do this in a consistent order. To do this, Python uses something called "method resolution order" (MRO) and an algorithm called C3 to get it straight.

Because the MRO is complex and a well-defined algorithm is used, Python can't leave it to you to get it right. That'd be annoying, wouldn't it? Instead, Python gives you the super() function, which handles all this for you in the places that you need the altering type of actions demonstrated in Child.altered above. With super(), you don't have to worry about getting this right, and Python will find the right function for you.

Using super() with __init__

The most common use of super() is actually in __init__ functions in base classes. This is usually the only place where you need to do some things in a child, then complete the initialization in the parent. Here's a quick example of doing that in the Child from these examples:

```
class Child(Parent):

    def __init__(self, stuff):
        self.stuff = stuff
        super(Child, self).__init__()
```

This is pretty much the same as the Child.altered example above, except I'm setting some variables in the __init__ before having the Parent initialize with its Parent.__init__.

Composition

Inheritance is useful, but another way to do the exact same thing is just to *use* other classes and modules, rather than rely on implicit inheritance. If you look at the three ways to exploit inheritance, two of the three involve writing new code to replace or alter functionality. This can easily be replicated by just calling functions in another class. Here's an example of doing this:

ex44e.py

```
1    class Other(object):
2
3        def override(self):
4            print "OTHER override()"
5
6        def implicit(self):
7            print "OTHER implicit()"
8
9        def altered(self):
10            print "OTHER altered()"
11
12   class Child(object):
13
14       def __init__(self):
15           self.other = Other()
16
17       def implicit(self):
18           self.other.implicit()
19
20       def override(self):
21           print "CHILD override()"
22
23       def altered(self):
24           print "CHILD, BEFORE OTHER altered()"
25           self.other.altered()
26           print "CHILD, AFTER OTHER altered()"
27
28   son = Child()
29
30   son.implicit()
31   son.override()
32   son.altered()
```

In this code I'm not using the name Parent, since there is *not* a parent-child is-a relationship. This is a has-a relationship, where Child has-a Other that it uses to get its work done. When I run this, I get the following output:

Exercise 44e Session

```
$ python ex44e.py
OTHER implicit()
CHILD override()
CHILD, BEFORE OTHER altered()
```

```
OTHER altered()
CHILD, AFTER OTHER altered()
```

You can see that most of the code in `Child` and `Other` is the same to accomplish the same thing. The only difference is that I had to define a `Child.implicit` function to do that one action. I could then ask myself if I need this `Other` to be a class, and could I just make it into a module named `other.py`?

When to Use Inheritance or Composition

The question of inheritance versus composition comes down to an attempt to solve the problem of reusable code. You don't want to have duplicated code all over your software, since that's not clean and efficient. Inheritance solves this problem by creating a mechanism for you to have implied features in base classes. Composition solves this by giving you modules and the ability to simply call functions in other classes.

If both solutions solve the problem of reuse, then which one is appropriate in which situations? The answer is incredibly subjective, but I'll give you my three guidelines for when to do which:

1. Avoid multiple inheritance at all costs, as it's too complex to be useful reliably. If you're stuck with it, then be prepared to know the class hierarchy and spend time finding where everything is coming from.

2. Use composition to package up code into modules that are used in many different unrelated places and situations.

3. Use inheritance only when there are clearly related reusable pieces of code that fit under a single common concept or if you have to because of something you're using.

However, do not be a slave to these rules. The thing to remember about object-oriented programming is that it is entirely a social convention programmers have created to package and share code. Because it's a social convention, but one that's codified in Python, you may be forced to avoid these rules because of the people you work with. In that case, find out how they use things and then just adapt to the situation.

Study Drills

There is only one Study Drill for this exercise because it is a big exercise. Go and read http://www.python.org/dev/peps/pep-0008 and start trying to use it in your code. You'll notice that some of it is different from what you've been learning in this book, but now you should be able to understand their recommendations and use them in your own code. The rest of the code in this book may or may not follow these guidelines, depending on if it makes the code more confusing. I suggest you also do this, as comprehension is more important than impressing everyone with your knowledge of esoteric style rules.

Common Student Questions

How do I get better at solving problems that I haven't seen before?
The only way to get better at solving problems is to solve as many problems as you can *by yourself*. Typically people hit a difficult problem and then rush out to find an answer. This is fine when you have to get things done, but if you have the time to solve it yourself, then take that time. Stop and bang your head against the problem for as long as possible, trying every possible thing, until you solve it or give up. After that, the answers you find will be more satisfying and you'll eventually get better at solving problems.

Aren't objects just copies of classes?
In some languages (like JavaScript), that is true. These are called prototype languages and there are not many differences between objects and classes other than usage. In Python, however, classes act as templates that "mint" new objects, similar to how coins were minted using a die (template).

You Make a Game

You need to start learning to feed yourself. Hopefully, as you have worked through this book, you have learned that all the information you need is on the internet. You just have to go search for it. The only thing you have been missing are the right words and what to look for when you search. Now you should have a sense of it, so it's about time you struggled through a big project and tried to get it working.

Here are your requirements:

1. Make a different game from the one I made.

2. Use more than one file, and use `import` to use them. Make sure you know what that is.

3. Use *one class per room* and give the classes names that fit their purpose (like GoldRoom, KoiPondRoom).

4. Your runner will need to know about these rooms, so make a class that runs them and knows about them. There's plenty of ways to do this, but consider having each room return what room is next or setting a variable of what room is next.

Other than that, I leave it to you. Spend a whole week on this and make it the best game you can. Use classes, functions, dicts, lists—anything you can to make it nice. The purpose of this lesson is to teach you how to structure classes that need other classes inside other files.

Remember, I'm not telling you *exactly* how to do this, because you have to do this yourself. Go figure it out. Programming is problem solving, and that means trying things, experimenting, failing, scrapping your work, and trying again. When you get stuck, ask for help and show people your code. If they are mean to you, ignore them, and focus on the people who are not mean and offer to help. Keep working it and cleaning it until it's good, then show it some more.

Good luck, and see you in a week with your game.

Evaluating Your Game

In this exercise, you will evaluate the game you just made. Maybe you got partway through it and you got stuck. Maybe you got it working but just barely. Either way, we're going to go through a bunch of things you should know now and make sure you covered them in your game. We're going to study how to properly format a class, common conventions in using classes, and a lot of "textbook" knowledge.

Why would I have you try to do it yourself and then show you how to do it right? From now on in the book, I'm going to try to make you self-sufficient. I've been holding your hand mostly this whole time, and I can't do that for much longer. I'm now instead going to give you things to do, have you do them on your own, and then give you ways to improve what you did.

You will struggle at first and probably be very frustrated, but stick with it and eventually you will build a mind for solving problems. You will start to find creative solutions to problems rather than just copy solutions out of textbooks.

Function Style

All the other rules I've taught you about how to make a function nice apply here, but add these things:

- For various reasons, programmers call functions that are part of classes methods. It's mostly marketing but just be warned that every time you say "function" they'll annoyingly correct you and say "method." If they get too annoying, just ask them to demonstrate the mathematical basis that determines how a "method" is different from a "function," and they'll shut up.

- When you work with classes, much of your time is spent talking about making the class "do things." Instead of naming your functions after what the function does, instead name it as if it's a command you are giving to the class. For example, pop essentially says, "Hey list, pop this off." It isn't called remove_from_end_of_list because, even though that's what it does, that's not a *command* to a list.

- Keep your functions small and simple. For some reason, when people start learning about classes, they forget this.

Class Style

- Your class should use "camel case" like SuperGoldFactory rather than super_gold_factory.

- Try not to do too much in your __init__ functions. It makes them harder to use.

- Your other functions should use "underscore format" so write my_awesome_hair and not myawesomehair or MyAwesomeHair.

- Be consistent in how you organize your function arguments. If your class has to deal with users, dogs, and cats, keep that order throughout unless it really doesn't make sense. If you have one function that takes (dog, cat, user) and the other takes (user, cat, dog), it'll be hard to use.

- Try not to use variables that come from the module or globals. They should be fairly self-contained.

- A foolish consistency is the hobgoblin of little minds. Consistency is good, but foolishly following some idiotic mantra because everyone else does is bad style. Think for yourself.

- Always, *always* have `class Name(object)` format or else you will be in big trouble.

Code Style

- Give your code vertical space so people can read it. You will find some very bad programmers who are able to write reasonable code but who do not add *any* spaces. This is bad style in any language because the human eye and brain use space and vertical alignment to scan and separate visual elements. Not having space is the same as giving your code an awesome camouflage paint job.

- If you can't read it out loud, it's probably hard to read. If you are having a problem making something easy to use, try reading it out loud. Not only does this force you to slow down and really read it, but it also helps you find difficult passages and things to change for readability.

- Try to do what other people are doing in Python until you find your own style.

- Once you find your own style, do not be a jerk about it. Working with other people's code is part of being a programmer, and other people have really bad taste. Trust me, you will probably have really bad taste too and not even realize it.

- If you find someone who writes code in a style you like, try writing something that mimics that style.

Good Comments

- There are programmers who will tell you that your code should be readable enough that you do not need comments. They'll then tell you in their most official sounding voice, "Ergo one should never write comments. QED." Those programmers are either consultants who get paid more if other people can't use their code or incompetents who tend to never work with other people. Ignore them and write comments.

- When you write comments, describe *why* you are doing what you are doing. The code already says how, but why you did things the way you did is more important.

- When you write doc comments for your functions, make the comments documentation for someone who will have to use your code. You do not have to go crazy, but a nice little sentence about what someone can do with that function helps a lot.

- Finally, while comments are good, too many are bad, and you have to maintain them. Keep your comments relatively short and to the point, and if you change a function, review the comment to make sure it's still correct.

Evaluate Your Game

I want you to now pretend you are me. Adopt a very stern look, print out your code, and take a red pen and mark every mistake you find, including anything from this exercise and from other guidelines you've read so far. Once you are done marking your code up, I want you to fix everything you came up with. Then repeat this a couple of times, looking for anything that could be better. Use all the tricks I've given you to break your code down into the smallest tiniest little analysis you can.

The purpose of this exercise is to train your attention to detail on classes. Once you are done with this bit of code, find someone else's code and do the same thing. Go through a printed copy of some part of it and point out all the mistakes and style errors you find. Then fix it and see if your fixes can be done without breaking that program.

I want you to do nothing but evaluate and fix code for the week. Your own code and other people's. It'll be pretty hard work, but when you are done, your brain will be wired tight like a boxer's hands.

A Project Skeleton

This will be where you start learning how to set up a good project "skeleton" directory. This skeleton directory will have all the basics you need to get a new project up and running. It will have your project layout, automated tests, modules, and install scripts. When you go to make a new project, just copy this directory to a new name and edit the files to get started.

Installing Python Packages

Before you can begin this exercise, you need to install some software for Python by using a tool called "pip" to install new modules. Here's the problem though. You are at a point where it's difficult for me to help you do that and keep this book sane and clean. There are so many ways to install software on so many computers that I'd have to spend 10 pages walking you through every step, and let me tell you I am a lazy guy.

Rather than tell you how to do it exactly, I'm going to tell you what you should install, and then tell you to figure it out and get it working. This will be really good for you, since it will open a whole world of software you can use that other people have released to the world.

Install the following Python packages:

1. pip from http://pypi.python.org/pypi/pip

2. distribute from http://pypi.python.org/pypi/distribute

3. nose from http://pypi.python.org/pypi/nose

4. virtualenv from http://pypi.python.org/pypi/virtualenv

Do not just download these packages and install them by hand. Instead, see how other people recommend you install these packages and use them for your particular system. The process will be different for most versions of Linux, OSX, and definitely different for Windows.

I am warning you; this will be frustrating. In the business we call this "yak shaving." Yak shaving is any activity that is mind-numbingly, irritatingly boring and tedious that you have to do before you can do something else that's more fun. You want to create cool Python projects, but you can't do that until you set up a skeleton directory, but you can't set up a skeleton directory until you install some packages, but you can't install packages until you install package installers, and you can't install package installers until you figure out how your system installs software in general, and so on.

Struggle through this anyway. Consider it your trial by annoyance to get into the programmer club. Every programmer has to do these annoying, tedious tasks before they can do something cool.

NOTE: Sometimes the Python installer does not add the C:\Python27\Script to the system PATH. If this is the case for you, go back and add this to the path just like you did for C:\Python27 in Exercise 0, with

`[Environment]::SetEnvironmentVariable("Path",`

`"$env:Path;C:\Python27\Scripts", "User")`

Creating the Skeleton Project Directory

First, create the structure of your skeleton directory with these commands:

```
$ mkdir projects
$ cd projects/
$ mkdir skeleton
$ cd skeleton
$ mkdir bin
$ mkdir NAME
$ mkdir tests
$ mkdir docs
```

I use a directory named projects to store all the various things I'm working on. Inside that directory, I have my skeleton directory that I put the basis of my projects into. The directory NAME will be renamed to whatever you are calling your project's main module when you use the skeleton.

Next we need to set up some initial files. Here's how you do that on Linux/OSX:

```
$ touch NAME/__init__.py
$ touch tests/__init__.py
```

Here's the same thing on Windows PowerShell:

```
$ new-item -type file NAME/__init__.py
$ new-item -type file tests/__init__.py
```

That creates an empty Python module directories we can put our code in. Then we need to create a setup.py file we can use to install our project later, if we want:

setup.py

```
1    try:
2        from setuptools import setup
```

```
3    except ImportError:
4        from distutils.core import setup
5
6    config = {
7        'description': 'My Project',
8        'author': 'My Name',
9        'url': 'URL to get it at.',
10       'download_url': 'Where to download it.',
11       'author_email': 'My email.',
12       'version': '0.1',
13       'install_requires': ['nose'],
14       'packages': ['NAME'],
15       'scripts': [],
16       'name': 'projectname'
17   }
18
19   setup(**config)
```

Edit this file so that it has your contact information and is ready to go for when you copy it. Finally you will want a simple skeleton file for tests named tests/NAME_tests.py:

NAME_tests.py

```
1    from nose.tools import *
2    import NAME
3
4    def setup():
5        print "SETUP!"
6
7    def teardown():
8        print "TEAR DOWN!"
9
10   def test_basic():
11       print "I RAN!"
```

Final Directory Structure

When you are done setting all this up, your directory should look like mine here:

```
$ ls -R
NAME                bin             docs            setup.py            tests

./NAME:
__init__.py

./bin:

./docs:

./tests:
NAME_tests.py    __init__.py
```

This is on Unix, but the structure is the same on Windows. Here's how it would look if I were to draw it out as a tree:

```
setup.py
NAME/
     __init__.py
bin/
docs/
tests/
     NAME_tests.py
     __init__.py
```

And, from now on, you should run your commands that work with this directory from this point. If you can't do `ls -R` and see this same structure, then you are in the wrong place. For example, people commonly go into the `tests/` directory to try to run files there, which won't work. To run your application's tests, you would need to be *above* `tests/` and this location I have above. Say you try this:

```
$ cd tests/    # WRONG! WRONG! WRONG!
$ nosetests

----------------------------------------------------------------------
Ran 0 tests in 0.000s

OK
```

That is *wrong*! You have to be above tests, so assuming you made this mistake, you would fix it by doing this:

```
$ cd ..    # get out of tests/
$ ls       # CORRECT! you are now in the right spot
NAME            bin             docs            setup.py        tests
$ nosetests
.
----------------------------------------------------------------------
Ran 1 test in 0.004s

OK
```

Remember this, because people make this mistake quite frequently.

Testing Your Setup

After you get all that installed, you should be able to do this:

```
$ nosetests
.
```

```
-----------------------------------------------------------------
Ran 1 test in 0.007s

OK
```

I'll explain what this nosetests thing is doing in the next exercise, but for now if you do not see that, you probably got something wrong. Make sure you put __init__.py files in your NAME and tests directories and make sure you got tests/NAME_tests.py right.

Using the Skeleton

You are now done with most of your yak shaving. Whenever you want to start a new project, just do this:

1. Make a copy of your skeleton directory. Name it after your new project.

2. Rename (move) the NAME module to be the name of your project or whatever you want to call your root module.

3. Edit your setup.py to have all the information for your project.

4. Rename tests/NAME_tests.py to also have your module name.

5. Double check it's all working by using nosetests again.

6. Start coding.

Required Quiz

This exercise doesn't have Study Drills but a quiz you should complete:

1. Read about how to use all the things you installed.

2. Read about the setup.py file and all it has to offer. Warning: it is not a very well-written piece of software, so it will be very strange to use.

3. Make a project and start putting code into the module, then get the module working.

4. Put a script in the bin directory that you can run. Read about how you can make a Python script that's runnable for your system.

5. Mention the bin script you created in your setup.py so that it gets installed.

6. Use your setup.py to install your own module and make sure it works, then use pip to uninstall it.

Common Student Questions

Do these instructions work on Windows?
They should, but depending on the version of Windows, you may need to struggle with the setup a bit to get it working. Just keep researching and trying it until you get it, or see if you can ask a more experienced Python+Windows friend to help out.

It seems I can't run nosetests on Windows.
Sometimes the Python installer does not add the C:\Python27\Script to the system PATH. If this is the case for you, go back and add this to the path just like you did for C:\Python27 in Exercise 0.

What do I put in the config dictionary in my setup.py?
Make sure you read the documentation for distutils at http://docs.python.org/distutils/setupscript .html.

I can't seem to load the NAME module and just get an ImportError.
Make sure you made the NAME/__init__.py file. If you're on Windows, make sure you didn't accidentally name it NAME/__init__.py.txt, which happens by default with some editors.

Why do we need a bin/ folder at all?
This is just a standard place to put scripts that are run on the command line, not a place to put modules.

Do you have a real-world example project?
There are many projects written in Python that do this, but try this simple one I created: https:// gitorious.org/python-modargs.

My nosetests run only shows one test being run. Is that right?
Yes, that's what my output shows too.

Automated Testing

Having to type commands into your game over and over to make sure it's working is annoying. Wouldn't it be better to write little pieces of code that test your code? Then when you make a change or add a new thing to your program, you just "run your tests" and the tests make sure things are still working. These automated tests won't catch all your bugs, but they will cut down on the time you spend repeatedly typing and running your code.

Every exercise after this one will not have a WYSS section, but instead it will have a What You Should Test section. You will be writing automated tests for all your code starting now, and this will hopefully make you an even better programmer.

I won't try to explain why you should write automated tests. I will only say that you are trying to be a programmer, and programmers automate boring and tedious tasks. Testing a piece of software is definitely boring and tedious, so you might as well write a little bit of code to do it for you.

That should be all the explanation you need because *your* reason for writing unit tests is to make your brain stronger. You have gone through this book writing code to do things. Now you are going to take the next leap and write code that knows about other code you have written. This process of writing a test that runs some code you have written *forces* you to understand clearly what you have just written. It solidifies in your brain exactly what it does and why it works and gives you a new level of attention to detail.

Writing a Test Case

We're going to take a very simple piece of code and write one simple test. We're going to base this little test on a new project from your project skeleton.

First, make a ex47 project from your project skeleton. Here are the steps you would take. I'm going to give these instructions in English rather than show you how to type them so that *you* have to figure it out.

1. Copy skeleton to ex47.

2. Rename everything with NAME to ex47.

3. Change the word NAME in all the files to ex47.

4. Finally, remove all the *.pyc files to make sure you're clean.

Refer back to Exercise 46 if you get stuck, and if you can't do this easily, then maybe practice it a few times.

NOTE: Remember that you run the command nosetests to run the tests. You can run them with python ex46_tests.py, but it won't work as easily and you'll have to do it for each test file.

Next, create a simple file ex47/game.py where you can put the code to test. This will be a very silly little class that we want to test with this code in it:

game.py

```
1    class Room(object):
2
3        def __init__(self, name, description):
4            self.name = name
5            self.description = description
6            self.paths = {}
7
8        def go(self, direction):
9            return self.paths.get(direction, None)
10
11        def add_paths(self, paths):
12            self.paths.update(paths)
```

Once you have that file, change the unit test skeleton to this:

ex47_tests.py

```
1    from nose.tools import *
2    from ex47.game import Room
3
4
5    def test_room():
6        gold = Room("GoldRoom",
7                    """This room has gold in it you can grab. There's a
8                    door to the north.""")
9        assert_equal(gold.name, "GoldRoom")
10       assert_equal(gold.paths, {})
11
12   def test_room_paths():
13       center = Room("Center", "Test room in the center.")
14       north = Room("North", "Test room in the north.")
15       south = Room("South", "Test room in the south.")
16
17       center.add_paths({'north': north, 'south': south})
18       assert_equal(center.go('north'), north)
19       assert_equal(center.go('south'), south)
20
21   def test_map():
22       start = Room("Start", "You can go west and down a hole.")
23       west = Room("Trees", "There are trees here, you can go east.")
24       down = Room("Dungeon", "It's dark down here, you can go up.")
```

```
25
26          start.add_paths({'west': west, 'down': down})
27          west.add_paths({'east': start})
28          down.add_paths({'up': start})
29
30          assert_equal(start.go('west'), west)
31          assert_equal(start.go('west').go('east'), start)
32          assert_equal(start.go('down').go('up'), start)
```

This file imports the Room class you made in the ex47.game module so that you can do tests on it. There is then a set of tests that are functions starting with test_. Inside each test case, there's a bit of code that makes a room or a set of rooms and then makes sure the rooms work the way you expect them to work. It tests out the basic room features, then the paths, then tries out a whole map.

The important functions here are assert_equal, which makes sure that variables you have set or paths you have built in a room are actually what you think they are. If you get the wrong result, then nosetests will print out an error message so you can go figure it out.

Testing Guidelines

Follow this general loose set of guidelines when making your tests:

1. Test files go in tests/ and are named BLAH_tests.py; otherwise nosetests won't run them. This also keeps your tests from clashing with your other code.

2. Write one test file for each module you make.

3. Keep your test cases (functions) short, but do not worry if they are a bit messy. Test cases are usually kind of messy.

4. Even though test cases are messy, try to keep them clean and remove any repetitive code you can. Create helper functions that get rid of duplicate code. You will thank me later when you make a change and then have to change your tests. Duplicated code will make changing your tests more difficult.

5. Finally, do not get too attached to your tests. Sometimes, the best way to redesign something is to just delete it and start over.

What You Should See

Exercise 47 Session

```
$ nosetests
...
----------------------------------------------------------------------
```

Ran 3 tests in 0.008s

OK

That's what you should see if everything is working right. Try causing an error to see what that looks like and then fix it.

Study Drills

1.   Go read about nosetests more, and also read about alternatives.

2.   Learn about Python's "doc tests" and see if you like them better.

3.   Make your room more advanced, and then use it to rebuild your game yet again. This time, unit test as you go.

Common Student Questions

I get a syntax error when I run nosetests.
If you get that, then look at what the error says and fix that line of code or the ones above it. Tools like nosetests are running your code and the test code, so they will find syntax errors the same as running Python will.

I can't import ex47.game.
Make sure you create the ex47/__init__.py file. Refer to Exercise 46 again to see how it's done. If that's not the problem, then do this on OSX/Linux:

```
export PYTHONPATH=.
```

And do this on Windows:

```
$env:PYTHONPATH = "$env:PYTHONPATH;."
```

Finally, make sure you're running other tests with nosetests, not with just Python.

I get UserWarning when I run nosetests.
You probably have two versions of Python installed or you aren't using distribute. Go back and install distribute or pip, as I describe in Exercise 46.

Advanced User Input

Your game probably works well, but your user input system isn't very robust. Each room needed its own very exact set of phrases that only worked if your player typed them perfectly. What you'd rather have is a device that lets users type phrases in various ways. For example, we'd like to have all these phrases work the same:

- Open door.

- Open the door.

- Go through the door.

These two phrases should also work the same:

- Punch bear.

- Punch the bear in the face.

It should be alright for a user to write something a lot like English for your game and have your game figure out what it means. To do this, we're going to write a module that does just that. This module will have a few classes that work together to handle user input and convert it into something your game can work with reliably. A simplified version of English can use these rules:

- Words separated by spaces.

- Sentences composed of the words.

- Grammar that structures the sentences into meaning.

That means the best place to start is figuring out how to get words from the user and what kinds of words those are.

Our Game Lexicon

In our game, we have to create a lexicon of words:

- **Direction words.** North, south, east, west, down, up, left, right, back.

- **Verbs.** Go, stop, kill, eat.

- **Stop words.** The, in, of, from, at, it.

- **Nouns.** Door, bear, princess, cabinet.

- **Numbers.** Any string of 0 through 9 characters.

When we get to nouns, we have a slight problem, since each room could have a different set of nouns, but let's just pick this small set to work with for now and improve it later.

Breaking Up a Sentence

Once we have our lexicon of words, we need a way to break up sentences so that we can figure out what they are. In our case, we've defined a sentence as "words separated by spaces," so we really just need to do this:

```
stuff = raw_input('> ')
words = stuff.split()
```

That's really all we'll worry about for now, but this will work really well for quite a while.

Lexicon Tuples

Once we know how to break up a sentence into words, we just have to go through the list of words and figure out what "type" they are. To do that, we're going to use a handy little Python structure called a "tuple." A tuple is nothing more than a list that you can't modify. It's created by putting data inside two () with a comma, like a list:

```
first_word = ('direction', 'north')
second_word = ('verb', 'go')
sentence = [first_word, second_word]
```

This creates a pair (TYPE, WORD) that lets you look at the word and do things with it.

This is just an example, but that's basically the end result. You want to take raw input from the user, carve it into words with `split`, then analyze those words to identify their type, and finally make a sentence out of them.

Scanning Input

Now you are ready to write your scanner. This scanner will take a string of raw input from a user and return a sentence that's composed of a list of tuples with the (TOKEN, WORD) pairings. If a word isn't part of the lexicon, then it should still return the WORD but set the TOKEN to an error token. These error tokens will tell users they messed up.

Here's where it gets fun. I'm not going to tell you how to do this. Instead I'm going to write a `unit test`, and you are going to write the scanner so that the unit test works.

Exceptions and Numbers

There is one tiny thing I will help you with first, and that's converting numbers. In order to do this, though, we're going to cheat and use exceptions. An exception is an error that you get from some function you may have run. What happens is your function "raises" an exception when it encounters an error, then you have to handle that exception. For example, say you type this into Python:

```
~/projects/simplegame $ python
Python 2.6.5 (r265:79063, Apr 16 2010, 13:57:41)
[GCC 4.4.3] on linux2
Type "help", "copyright", "credits" or "license" for more information.
>>> int("hell")
Traceback (most recent call last):
  File "<stdin>", line 1, in <module>
ValueError: invalid literal for int() with base 10: 'hell'
>>
```

That ValueError is an exception that the int() function threw because what you handed int() is not a number. The int() function could have returned a value to tell you it had an error, but since it only returns integers, it'd have a hard time doing that. It can't return –1, since that's a number. Instead of trying to figure out what to return when there's an error, the int() function raises the ValueError exception and you deal with it.

You deal with an exception by using the try and except keywords:

```
def convert_number(s):
    try:
        return int(s)
    except ValueError:
        return None
```

You put the code you want to "try" inside the try block, and then you put the code to run for the error inside the except. In this case, we want to "try" to call int() on something that might be a number. If that has an error, then we "catch" it and return None.

In your scanner that you write, you should use this function to test if something is a number. You should also do it as the last thing you check for before declaring that word an error word.

What You Should Test

Here are the files from tests/lexicon_tests.py that you should use:

ex48.py

```
1    from nose.tools import *
2    from ex48 import lexicon
3
```

```
4
5    def test_directions():
6        assert_equal(lexicon.scan("north"), [('direction', 'north')])
7        result = lexicon.scan("north south east")
8        assert_equal(result, [('direction', 'north'),
9                              ('direction', 'south'),
10                             ('direction', 'east')])
11
12   def test_verbs():
13       assert_equal(lexicon.scan("go"), [('verb', 'go')])
14       result = lexicon.scan("go kill eat")
15       assert_equal(result, [('verb', 'go'),
16                             ('verb', 'kill'),
17                             ('verb', 'eat')])
18
19
20   def test_stops():
21       assert_equal(lexicon.scan("the"), [('stop', 'the')])
22       result = lexicon.scan("the in of")
23       assert_equal(result, [('stop', 'the'),
24                             ('stop', 'in'),
25                             ('stop', 'of')])
26
27
28   def test_nouns():
29       assert_equal(lexicon.scan("bear"), [('noun', 'bear')])
30       result = lexicon.scan("bear princess")
31       assert_equal(result, [('noun', 'bear'),
32                             ('noun', 'princess')])
33
34   def test_numbers():
35       assert_equal(lexicon.scan("1234"), [('number', 1234)])
36       result = lexicon.scan("3 91234")
37       assert_equal(result, [('number', 3),
38                             ('number', 91234)])
39
40
41   def test_errors():
42       assert_equal(lexicon.scan("ASDFADFASDF"), [('error', 'ASDFADFASDF')])
43       result = lexicon.scan("bear IAS princess")
44       assert_equal(result, [('noun', 'bear'),
45                             ('error', 'IAS'),
46                             ('noun', 'princess')])
```

Remember that you will want to make a new project with your skeleton, type in this test case (do not copy-paste!) and write your scanner so that the test runs. Focus on the details and make sure everything works right.

Design Hints

Focus on getting one test working at a time. Keep this simple and just put all the words in your lexicon in lists that are in your `lexicon.py` module. Do not modify the input list of words, but instead make your own new list with your lexicon tuples in it. Also, use the `in` keyword with these lexicon lists to check if a word is in the lexicon. Use a dictionary in your solution.

Study Drills

1. Improve the unit test to make sure you cover more of the lexicon.

2. Add to the lexicon and then update the unit test.

3. Make sure your scanner handles user input in any capitalization and case. Update the test to make sure this actually works.

4. Find another way to convert the number.

5. My solution was 37 lines long. Is yours longer? Shorter?

Common Student Questions

Why do I keep getting `ImportErrors`?
Import errors are caused by usually four things: (1) you didn't make a `__init__.py` in a directory that has modules in it, (2) you are in the wrong directory, (3) you are importing the wrong module because you spelled it wrong, (4) your PYTHONPATH isn't set to `.` so you can't load modules from your current directory.

What's the difference between `try-except` and `if-else`?
The `try-expect` construct is only used for handling exceptions that modules can throw. It should *never* be used as an alternative to `if-else`.

Is there a way to keep the game running while the user is waiting to type?
I'm assuming you want to have a monster attack users if they don't react quick enough. It is possible, but it involves modules and techniques that are outside of this book's domain.

Making Sentences

What we should be able to get from our little game lexicon scanner is a list that looks like this:

```
>>> from ex48 import lexicon
>>> print lexicon.scan("go north")
[('verb', 'go'), ('direction', 'north')]
>>> print lexicon.scan("kill the princess")
[('verb', 'kill'), ('stop', 'the'), ('noun', 'princess')]
>>> print lexicon.scan("eat the bear")
[('verb', 'eat'), ('stop', 'the'), ('noun', 'bear')]
>>> print lexicon.scan("open the door and smack the bear in the nose")
[('error', 'open'), ('stop', 'the'), ('noun', 'door'), ('error', 'and'),
('error', 'smack'), ('stop', 'the'), ('noun', 'bear'), ('stop', 'in'),
('stop', 'the'), ('error', 'nose')]
>>>
```

Now let us turn this into something the game can work with, which would be some kind of sentence class. If you remember grade school, a sentence can be a simple structure like:

Subject Verb Object

Obviously it gets more complex than that, and you probably did many days of annoying sentence graphs for English class. What we want is to turn the above lists of tuples into a nice sentence object that has a subject, verb, and object.

Match and Peek

To do this we need four tools:

1. A way to loop through the list of tuples. That's easy.

2. A way to "match" different types of tuples that we expect in our subject-verb-object setup.

3. A way to "peek" at a potential tuple so we can make some decisions.

4. A way to "skip" things we do not care about, like stop words.

We will be putting these functions in a file named ex48/parser.py in order to test it. We use the peek function to look at the next element in our tuple list, and then match to take one off and work with it. Let's take a look at a first peek function:

```
def peek(word_list):
    if word_list:
        word = word_list[0]
        return word[0]
    else:
        return None
```

Very easy. Now for the match function:

```
def match(word_list, expecting):
    if word_list:
        word = word_list.pop(0)

        if word[0] == expecting:
            return word
        else:
            return None
    else:
        return None
```

Again, very easy, and finally our skip function:

```
def skip(word_list, word_type):
    while peek(word_list) == word_type:
        match(word_list, word_type)
```

By now you should be able to figure out what these do. Make sure you understand them.

The Sentence Grammar

With our tools we can now begin to build sentence objects from our list of tuples. We use the following process:

1. Identify the next word with peek.

2. If that word fits in our grammar, we call a function to handle that part of the grammar—say, parse_subject.

3. If it doesn't, we raise an error, which you will learn about in this lesson.

4. When we're all done, we should have a sentence object to work with in our game.

The best way to demonstrate this is to give you the code to read, but here's where this exercise is different from the previous one: You will write the test for the parser code I give you. Rather than giving you the test so you can write the code, I will give you the code, and you have to write the test.

Here's the code that I wrote for parsing simple sentences by using the ex48.lexicon module:

ex49.py

```
1    class ParserError(Exception):
2        pass
3
4
5    class Sentence(object):
6
7        def __init__(self, subject, verb, object):
8            # remember we take ('noun','princess') tuples and convert them
9            self.subject = subject[1]
10           self.verb = verb[1]
11           self.object = object[1]
12
13
14   def peek(word_list):
15       if word_list:
16           word = word_list[0]
17           return word[0]
18       else:
19           return None
20
21
22   def match(word_list, expecting):
23       if word_list:
24           word = word_list.pop(0)
25
26           if word[0] == expecting:
27               return word
28           else:
29               return None
30       else:
31           return None
32
33
34   def skip(word_list, word_type):
35       while peek(word_list) == word_type:
36           match(word_list, word_type)
37
38
39   def parse_verb(word_list):
40       skip(word_list, 'stop')
41
42       if peek(word_list) == 'verb':
43           return match(word_list, 'verb')
44       else:
45           raise ParserError("Expected a verb next.")
```

```
46
47
48   def parse_object(word_list):
49       skip(word_list, 'stop')
50       next = peek(word_list)
51
52       if next == 'noun':
53           return match(word_list, 'noun')
54       if next == 'direction':
55           return match(word_list, 'direction')
56       else:
57           raise ParserError("Expected a noun or direction next.")
58
59
60   def parse_subject(word_list, subj):
61       verb = parse_verb(word_list)
62       obj = parse_object(word_list)
63
64       return Sentence(subj, verb, obj)
65
66
67   def parse_sentence(word_list):
68       skip(word_list, 'stop')
69
70       start = peek(word_list)
71
72       if start == 'noun':
73           subj = match(word_list, 'noun')
74           return parse_subject(word_list, subj)
75       elif start == 'verb':
76           # assume the subject is the player then
77           return parse_subject(word_list, ('noun', 'player'))
78       else:
79           raise ParserError("Must start with subject, object, or verb not: %s" % start)
```

A Word on Exceptions

You briefly learned about exceptions but not how to raise them. This code demonstrates how to do that with the ParserError at the top. Notice that it uses classes to give it the type of Exception. Also notice the use of the raise keyword to raise the exception.

In your tests, you will want to work with these exceptions, which I'll show you how to do.

What You Should Test

For Exercise 49, write a complete test that confirms everything in this code is working. Put the test in `tests/parser_tests.py`, similar to the test file from the last exercise. That includes making exceptions happen by giving it bad sentences.

Check for an exception by using the function `assert_raises` from the nose documentation. Learn how to use this so you can write a test that is *expected* to fail, which is very important in testing. Learn about this function (and others) by reading the nose documentation.

When you are done, you should know how this bit of code works and how to write a test for other people's code, even if they do not want you to. Trust me, it's a very handy skill to have.

Study Drills

1. Change the `parse_` methods and try to put them into a class rather than be just methods. Which design do you like better?

2. Make the parser more error resistant so that you can avoid annoying your users if they type words your lexicon doesn't understand.

3. Improve the grammar by handling more things like numbers.

4. Think about how you might use this sentence class in your game to do more fun things with a user's input.

Common Student Questions

I can't seem to make `assert_raises` work right.
Make sure you are writing `assert_raises(exception, callable, parameters)` and *not* writing `assert_raises(exception, callable(parameters))`. Notice how the second form is calling the function then passing the result to `assert_raises`, which is *wrong*. You have to pass the function to call *and* its arguments to `assert_raises` instead.

Your First Website

These final three exercises will be very hard, and you should take your time with them. In this first one, you'll build a simple web version of one of your games. Before you attempt this exercise, you *must* have completed Exercise 46 successfully and have a working pip installed such that you can install packages and know how to make a skeleton project directory. If you don't remember how to do this, go back to Exercise 46 and do it all over again.

Installing lpthw.web

Before creating your first web application, you'll first need to install the "web framework" called lpthw.web. The term "framework" generally means "some package that makes it easier for me to do something." In the world of web applications, people create "web frameworks" to compensate for the difficult problems they've encountered when making their own sites. They share these common solutions in the form of a package you can download to bootstrap your own projects.

In our case, we'll be using the lpthw.web framework, but there are many, many, *many* others you can choose from. For now, learn lpthw.web, then branch out to another one when you're ready (or just keep using lpthw.web since it's good enough).

Using pip, install lpthw.web:

```
$ sudo pip install lpthw.web
[sudo] password for zedshaw:
Downloading/unpacking lpthw.web
  Running setup.py egg_info for package lpthw.web

Installing collected packages: lpthw.web
  Running setup.py install for lpthw.web

Successfully installed lpthw.web
Cleaning up...
```

This will work on Linux and Mac OSX computers, but on Windows just drop the sudo part of the pip install command and it should work. If not, go back to Exercise 46 and make sure you can do it reliably.

WARNING! Other Python programmers will warn you that lpthw.web is just a fork of another web framework called web.py and that web.py has too much "magic." If they say this, point out to them that Google App Engine originally used web.py, and not a single Python programmer complained that it had too much magic, because they all worked at Google. If it's good enough for Google, then it's good enough for you to get started. Then, just get back to learning to code and ignore their goal of indoctrination over education.

Make a Simple "Hello World" Project

Now you're going to make an initial very simple "Hello World" web application and project directory using lpthw.web. First, make your project directory:

```
$ cd projects
$ mkdir gothonweb
$ cd gothonweb
$ mkdir bin gothonweb tests docs templates
$ touch gothonweb/__init__.py
$ touch tests/__init__.py
```

You'll be taking the game from Exercise 43 and making it into a web application, so that's why you're calling it gothonweb. Before you do that, we need to create the most basic lpthw.web application possible. Put the following code into bin/app.py:

ex50.py

```
1    import web
2
3    urls = (
4      '/', 'index'
5    )
6
7    app = web.application(urls, globals())
8
9    class index:
10       def GET(self):
11           greeting = "Hello World"
12           return greeting
13
14   if __name__ == "__main__":
15       app.run()
```

Then run the application like this:

```
$ python bin/app.py
http://0.0.0.0:8080/
```

However, say you did this:

```
$ cd bin/   # WRONG! WRONG! WRONG!
$ python app.py  # WRONG! WRONG! WRONG!
```

Then you are doing it *wrong*. In all Python projects, you do not cd into a lower directory to run things. You stay at the top and run everything from there so that all of the system can access all the modules and files. Go reread Exercise 46 to understand a project layout and how to use it if you did this.

Finally, use your web browser and go to `http://localhost:8080`, and you should see two things. First, in your browser you'll see `Hello World!`. Second, you'll see your Terminal with new output like this:

```
$ python bin/app.py
http://0.0.0.0:8080/
127.0.0.1:59542 - - [13/Jun/2011 11:44:43] "http/1.1 GET /" - 200 OK
127.0.0.1:59542 - - [13/Jun/2011 11:44:43] "http/1.1 GET /favicon.ico" - 404 Not Found
```

Those are log messages that `lpthw.web` prints out so you can see that the server is working and what the browser is doing behind the scenes. The log messages help you debug and figure out when you have problems. For example, it's saying that your browser tried to get `/favicon.ico`, but that file didn't exist, so it returned the 404 Not Found status code.

I haven't explained the way *any* of this web stuff works yet, because I want to get you set up and ready to roll so that I can explain it better in the next two exercises. To accomplish this, I'll have you break your `lpthw.web` application in various ways and then restructure it so that you know how it's set up.

What's Going On?

Here's what's happening when your browser hits your application:

1. Your browser makes a network connection to your own computer, which is called `localhost` and is a standard way of saying "whatever my own computer is called on the network." It also uses port 8080.

2. Once it connects, it makes an HTTP request to the `bin/app.py` application and asks for the / URL, which is commonly the first URL on any website.

3. Inside `bin/app.py` you've got a list of URLs and what classes they match. The only one we have is the `'/'`, `'index'` mapping. This means that whenever someone goes to / with a browser, `lpthw.web` will find the `class index` and load it to handle the request.

4. Now that `lpthw.web` has found `class index` it calls the `index.GET` method on an instance of that class to actually handle the request. This function runs and simply returns a string for what `lpthw.web` should send to the browser.

5. Finally, `lpthw.web` has handled the request and sends this response to the browser, which is what you are seeing.

Make sure you really understand this. Draw up a diagram of how this information flows from your browser, to `lpthw.web`, then to `index.GET` and back to your browser.

Fixing Errors

First, delete line 11 where you assign the `greeting` variable; then hit refresh in your browser. You should see an error page now that gives you lots of information on how your application just exploded. You know that the variable `greeting` is now missing, but `lpthw.web` gives you this nice error page to track down exactly where. Do each of the following with this page:

1. Look at each of the `Local vars` outputs (click on them) and see if you can follow what variables it's talking about and where they are.

2. Look at the Request Information section and see if it matches anything you're already familiar with. This is information that your web browser is sending to your gothonweb application. You normally don't even know that it's sending this stuff, so now you get to see what it does.

3. Try breaking this simple application in other ways and explore what happens. Don't forget to also look at the logs being printed into your Terminal, as `lpthw.web` will put other stack traces and information there too.

Create Basic Templates

You can break your `lpthw.web` application, but did you notice that "Hello World" isn't a very good HTML page? This is a web application, and as such it needs a proper HTML response. To do that, you will create a simple template that says `Hello World!` in a big green font.

The first step is to create a `templates/index.html` file that looks like this:

```
                                                                    index.html
```

```
$def with (greeting)
<html>
```

```
    <head>
        <title>Gothons Of Planet Percal #25</title>
    </head>
<body>

$if greeting:
    I just wanted to say <em style="color: green; font-size: 2em;">$greeting</em>.
$else:
    <em>Hello</em> World!

</body>
</html>
```

If you know what HTML is, then this should look fairly familiar. If not, research HTML and try writing a few web pages by hand so you know how it works. This HTML file, however, is a *template*, which means that lpthw.web will fill in "holes" in the text depending on variables you pass in to the template. Every place you see $greeting will be a variable you'll pass to the template that alters its contents.

To make your bin/app.py do this, you need to add some code to tell lpthw.web where to load the template and to render it. Take that file and change it like this:

app.py

```
1    import web
2
3    urls = (
4      '/', 'Index'
5    )
6
7    app = web.application(urls, globals())
8
9    render = web.template.render('templates/')
10
11   class Index(object):
12       def GET(self):
13           greeting = "Hello World"
14           return render.index(greeting = greeting)
15
16   if __name__ == "__main__":
17       app.run()
```

Pay close attention to the new render variable and how I changed the last line of index.GET so it returns render.index(), passing in your greeting variable.

Once you have that in place, reload the web page in your browser and you should see a different message in green. You should also be able to do a View Source on the page in your browser to see that it is valid HTML.

This may have flown by you very fast, so let me explain how a template works:

1. In your bin/app.py you've added a new variable, render, which is a web.template.render object.

2. This render object knows how to load .html files out of the templates/ directory because you passed that to it as a parameter.

3. Later in your code, when the browser hits the index.GET like before, instead of just returning the string greeting, you call render.index and pass the greeting to it as a variable.

4. This render.index method is kind of a *magic* function where the render object sees that you're asking for index, goes into the templates/ directory, looks for a page named index.html, and then "renders" it, or converts it.

5. In the templates/index.html file you see the beginning definition that says this template takes a greeting parameter, just like a function. Also, just like Python this template is indentation sensitive, so make sure you get them right.

6. Finally, you have the HTML in templates/index.html that looks at the greeting variable and, if it's there, prints one message using the $greeting, or a default message.

To get deeper into this, change the greeting variable and the HTML to see what effect it has. Also create another template named templates/foo.html and render that using render.foo() instead of render.index(), like before. This will show you how the name of the function you call on render is just matched to an .html file in templates/.

Study Drills

1. Read the documentation at http://webpy.org, which is the same as the lpthw.web project.

2. Experiment with everything you can find there, including their example code.

3. Read about HTML5 and CSS3 and make some other .html and .css files for practice.

4. If you have a friend who knows Django and is willing to help you, then consider doing Exercises 50, 51, and 52 in Django instead to see what that's like.

Common Student Questions

I can't seem to connect to http://localhost:8080.
Try going to http://127.0.0.1:8080 instead.

What is the difference between `lpthw.web` and `web.py`?
No difference. I simply "locked" web.py at a particular version so that it would be consistent for students, then named it lpthw.web. Later versions of web.py might be different from this version.

I can't find `index.html` (or just about anything).
You probably are doing cd bin/ first and then trying to work with the project. Do not do this. All the commands and instructions assume you are one directory above bin/, so if you can't type python bin/app.py then you are in the wrong directory.

Why do we assign `greeting=greeting` when we call the template?
You are not assigning to greeting; you are setting a named parameter to give to the template. It's sort of an assignment, but it only affects the call to the template function.

I can't use port 8080 on my computer.
You probably have an antivirus program installed that is using that port. Try a different port.

After installing `lpthw.web`, I get `ImportError "No module named web"`.
You most likely have multiple versions of Python installed and are using the wrong one, or you didn't do the install correctly because of an old version of pip. Try uninstalling lpthw.web and reinstalling it. If that doesn't work, make triple sure you're using the right version of Python.

Getting Input from a Browser

While it's exciting to see the browser display Hello World!, it's even more exciting to let the user submit text to your application from a form. In this exercise, we'll improve our starter web application by using forms and storing information about users into their "sessions."

How the Web Works

Time for some boring stuff. You need to understand a bit more about how the web works before you can make a form. This description isn't complete, but it's accurate and will help you figure out what might be going wrong with your application. Also, creating forms will be easier if you know what they do.

I'll start with a simple diagram that shows you the different parts of a web request and how the information flows:

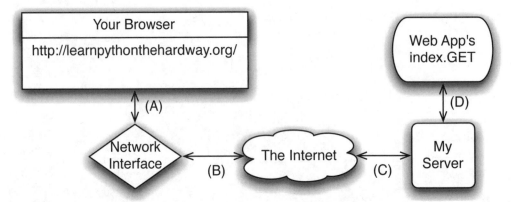

I've labeled the lines with letters so I can walk you through a regular request process:

1. You type in the URL http://learnpythonthehardway.org into your browser, and it sends the request out on line (A) to your computer's network interface.

2. Your request goes out over the internet on line (B) and then to the remote computer on line (C), where my server accepts the request.

3. Once my computer accepts it, my web application gets it on line (D), and my Python code runs the index.GET handler.

4. The response comes out of my Python server when I return it, and it goes back to your browser over line (D) again.

5. The server running this site takes the response off `line` (D) then sends it back over the internet on `line` (C).

6. The response from the server then comes off the internet on `line` (B), and your computer's network interface hands it to your browser on `line` (A).

7. Finally, your browser then displays the response.

In this description, there are a few terms you should know so that you have a common vocabulary to work with when talking about your web application:

Browser   The software that you're probably using every day. Most people don't know what a browser really does. They just call browsers "the internet." Its job is to take addresses (like http://learnpythonthehardway.org) you type into the URL bar, then use that information to make requests to the server at that address.

Address   This is normally a URL (uniform resource locator) like http://learnpythonthehardway .org and indicates where a browser should go. The first part (http) indicates the protocol you want to use—in this case, "hyper-text transport protocol." You can also try ftp://ibiblio .org to see how "File Transport Protocol" works. The second part (learnpythonthehardway .org) is the "hostname," or a human readable address you can remember and that maps to a number called an IP address, similar to a telephone number for a computer on the internet. Finally, URLs can have a trailing path like the "/book" part of http:// learnpythonthehardway.org/book, which indicates a file or some resource *on* the server to retrieve with a request. There are many other parts, but those are the main ones.

Connection   Once a browser knows what protocol you want to use (http), what server you want to talk to (learnpythonthehardway.org), and what resource on that server to get, it must make a connection. The browser simply asks your operating system (OS) to open a "port" to the computer—usually port 80. When it works, the OS hands back to your program something that works like a file but is actually sending and receiving bytes over the network wires between your computer and the other computer at "learnpythonthehardway .org." This is also the same thing that happens with http://localhost:8080, but in this case you're telling the browser to connect to your own computer (localhost) and use port 8080 rather than the default of 80. You could also do http://learnpythonthehardway .org:80 and get the same result, except you're explicitly saying to use port 80 instead of letting it be that by default.

Request   Your browser is connected using the address you gave. Now it needs to ask for the resource it wants (or you want) on the remote server. If you gave "/book" at the end of the URL, then you want the file (resource) at "/book"; most servers will use the real file / book/index.html, but pretend it doesn't exist. What the browser does to get this resource is send a *request* to the server. I won't get into exactly how it does this, but just understand that it has to send something to query the server for the request. The interesting thing is that these "resources" don't have to be files. For instance, when the browser in your application asks for something, the server is returning something your Python code generated.

Server   The server is the computer at the end of a browser's connection that knows how to answer your browser's requests for files/resources. Most web servers just send files, and that's actually the majority of traffic. But you're actually building a server in Python that knows how to take requests for resources and then return strings that you craft using Python. When you do this crafting, *you* are pretending to be a file to the browser, but really it's just code. As you can see from Exercise 50, it also doesn't take much code to create a response.

Response   This is the HTML (CSS, JavaScript, or images) your server wants to send back to the browser as the answer to the browser's request. In the case of files, it just reads them off the disk and sends them to the browser, but it wraps the contents of the disk in a special "header" so the browser knows what it's getting. In the case of your application, you're still sending the same thing, including the header, but you generate that data on the fly with your Python code.

That is the fastest crash course in how a web browser accesses information on servers on the internet. It should work well enough for you to understand this exercise, but if not, read about it as much as you can until you get it. A really good way to do that is to take the diagram and break different parts of the web application you did in Exercise 50. If you can break your web application in predictable ways using the diagram, you'll start to understand how it works.

How Forms Work

The best way to play with forms is to write some code that accepts form data and then see what you can do. Take your bin/app.py file and make it look like this:

form_test.py

```
1    import web
2
3    urls = (
4      '/hello', 'Index'
5    )
6
7
8    app = web.application(urls, globals())
9
10   render = web.template.render('templates/')
11
12   class Index(object):
13       def GET(self):
14           form = web.input(name="Nobody")
15           greeting = "Hello, %s" % form.name
16
```

```
17              return render.index(greeting = greeting)
18
19   if __name__ == "__main__":
20       app.run()
```

Restart it (hit CTRL-c and then run it again) to make sure it loads again; then with your browser go to http://localhost:8080/hello, which should display, "I just wanted to say Hello, Nobody." Next, change the URL in your browser to http://localhost:8080/hello?name=Frank, and you'll see it say, "Hello, Frank." Finally, change the name=Frank part to be your name. Now it's saying hello to you.

Let's break down the changes I made to your script.

1. Instead of just a string for greeting I'm now using web.input to get data from the browser. This function takes a key=value set of defaults, parses the ?name=Frank part of the URL you give it, and then returns a nice object for you to work with that represents those values.

2. I then construct the greeting from the new form.name attribute of the form object, which should be very familiar to you by now.

3. Everything else about the file is the same as before.

You're also not restricted to just one parameter on the URL. Change this example to give two variables like this: http://localhost:8080/hello?name=Frank&greet=Hola. Then change the code to get form.name and form.greet like this:

```
greeting = "%s, %s" % (form.greet, form.name)
```

After that, try the URL. Next, leave out the &greet=Hola part so that you can see the error you get. Since greet doesn't have a default value in web.input(name="Nobody"), it is a required field. Now go back and make it have a default in the web.input call to see how you fix this. Another thing you can do is set its default to greet=None so that you can check if it exists and then give a better error message, like this:

```
form = web.input(name="Nobody", greet=None)

if form.greet:
    greeting = "%s, %s" % (form.greet, form.name)
    return render.index(greeting = greeting)
else:
    return "ERROR: greet is required."
```

Creating HTML Forms

Passing the parameters on the URL works, but it's kind of ugly and not easy to use for regular people. What you really want is a "POST form," which is a special HTML file that has a <form> tag in it. This form will collect information from the user, then send it to your web application just like you did above.

Let's make a quick one so you can see how it works. Here's the new HTML file you need to create, in templates/hello_form.html:

hello_form.html

```
1    <html>
2        <head>
3            <title>Sample Web Form</title>
4        </head>
5    <body>
6
7    <h1>Fill Out This Form</h1>
8
9    <form action="/hello" method="POST">
10       A Greeting: <input type="text" name="greet">
11       <br/>
12       Your Name: <input type="text" name="name">
13       <br/>
14       <input type="submit">
15   </form>
16
17   </body>
18   </html>
```

You should then change bin/app.py to look like this:

post_form.py

```
1    import web
2
3    urls = (
4      '/hello', 'Index'
5    )
6
7    app = web.application(urls, globals())
8
9    render = web.template.render('templates/')
10
11   class Index(object):
12       def GET(self):
13           return render.hello_form()
14
15       def POST(self):
16           form = web.input(name="Nobody", greet="Hello")
```

```
17              greeting = "%s, %s" % (form.greet, form.name)
18              return render.index(greeting = greeting)
19
20  if __name__ == "__main__":
21      app.run()
```

Once you've got those written up, simply restart the web application again and hit it with your browser like before.

This time, you'll get a form asking you for "A Greeting" and "Your Name." When you hit the Submit button on the form, it will give you the same greeting you normally get, but this time look at the URL in your browser. See how it's http://localhost:8080/hello, even though you sent in parameters.

The part of the hello_form.html file that makes this work is the line with <form action="/hello" method="POST">. This tells your browser the following:

1. Collect data from the user using the form fields inside the form.

2. Send them to the server using a POST type of request, which is just another browser request that "hides" the form fields.

3. Send that to the /hello URL (as shown in the action="/hello" part).

You can then see how the two <input> tags match the names of the variables in your new code. Also notice that instead of just a GET method inside class index, I have another method, POST. This new application works as follows:

1. The browser first hits the web application at /hello but it sends a GET, so our index.GET function runs and returns the hello_form.

2. You fill out the form in the browser, and the browser does what the <form> says and sends the data as a POST.

3. The web application then runs the index.POST method rather than the index.GET method to handle this request.

4. This index.POST method then does what it normally does to send back the hello page like before. There's really nothing new in here; it's just moved into a new function.

As an exercise, go into the templates/index.html file and add a link *back* to just /hello so that you can keep filling out the form and seeing the results. Make sure you can explain how this link works and how it's letting you cycle between templates/index.html and templates/hello_form.html and what's being run inside this latest Python code.

Creating a Layout Template

When you work on your game in the next exercise, you'll need to make a bunch of little HTML pages. Writing a full web page each time will quickly become tedious. Luckily you can create a "layout" template or a kind of shell that will wrap all your other pages with common headers and footers. Good programmers try to reduce repetition, so layouts are essential for being a good programmer.

Change `templates/index.html` to be like this:

index_laid_out.html

```
$def with (greeting)

$if greeting:
    I just wanted to say <em style="color: green; font-size: 2em;">$greeting</em>.
$else:
    <em>Hello</em> World!
```

Then change `templates/hello_form.html` to be like this:

hello_form_laid_out.html

```
<h1>Fill Out This Form</h1>

<form action="/hello" method="POST">
    A Greeting: <input type="text" name="greet">
    <br/>
    Your Name: <input type="text" name="name">
    <br/>
    <input type="submit">
</form>
```

All we're doing is stripping out the "boilerplate" at the top and the bottom, which is always on every page. We'll put that back into a single `templates/layout.html` file that handles it for us from now on.

Once you have those changes, create a `templates/layout.html` file with this in it:

layout.html

```
$def with (content)

<html>
<head>
    <title>Gothons From Planet Percal #25</title>
</head>
<body>

$:content

</body>
</html>
```

This file looks like a regular template, except that it's going to be passed the *contents* of the other templates and used to *wrap* them. Anything you put in here doesn't need to be in the other templates. You should also pay attention to how $:content is written, since it's a little different from the other template variables.

The *final* step is to change the line that makes the render object to be this:

```
render = web.template.render('templates/', base="layout")
```

That tells lpthw.web to use the templates/layout.html file as the *base* template for all the other templates. Restart your application and then try to change the layout in interesting ways but without changing the other templates.

Writing Automated Tests for Forms

It's easy to test a web application with your browser by just hitting refresh, but come on, we're programmers here. Why do some repetitive task when we can write some code to test our application? What you're going to do next is write a little test for your web application form based on what you learned in Exercise 47. If you don't remember Exercise 47, read it again.

You need to do a bit of setup to make Python let you load your bin/app.py file for testing. When we get to Exercise 52 you'll change this, but for now create an empty bin/__init__.py file so Python thinks bin/ is a directory.

I've also created a simple little function for lpthw.web that lets you assert things about your web application's response, aptly named assert_response. Create the file tests/tools.py with these contents:

tools.py

```
1    from nose.tools import *
2    import re
3
4    def assert_response(resp, contains=None, matches=None, headers=None, status="200"):
5
6        assert status in resp.status, "Expected response %r not in %r" % (status, resp.status)
7
8        if status == "200":
9            assert resp.data, "Response data is empty."
10
11       if contains:
12           assert contains in resp.data, "Response does not contain %r" % contains
13
14       if matches:
15           reg = re.compile(matches)
16           assert reg.matches(resp.data), "Response does not match %r" % matches
17
```

```
18          if headers:
19              assert_equal(resp.headers, headers)
```

Once that's in place, you can write your automated test for the last version of the bin/app.py file you created. Create a new file named tests/app_tests.py with this:

app_tests.py

```
1    from nose.tools import *
2    from bin.app import app
3    from tests.tools import assert_response
4
5    def test_index():
6        # check that we get a 404 on the / URL
7        resp = app.request("/")
8        assert_response(resp, status="404")
9
10       # test our first GET request to /hello
11       resp = app.request("/hello")
12       assert_response(resp)
13
14       # make sure default values work for the form
15       resp = app.request("/hello", method="POST")
16       assert_response(resp, contains="Nobody")
17
18       # test that we get expected values
19       data = {'name': 'Zed', 'greet': 'Hola'}
20       resp = app.request("/hello", method="POST", data=data)
21       assert_response(resp, contains="Zed")
```

Finally, use nosetests to run this test setup and test your web application:

```
$ nosetests
.
----------------------------------------------------------------------
Ran 1 test in 0.059s

OK
```

What I'm doing here is I'm actually *importing* the whole application from the bin/app.py module, then running it manually. The lpthw.web framework has a very simple API for processing requests, which looks like this:

```
app.request(localpart='/', method='GET', data=None, host='0.0.0.0:8080',
            headers=None, https=False)
```

This means you can pass in the URL as the first parameter, then change the method of the request, as well as what form data you send, including the host and headers. This works without running an actual web server so you can do tests with automated tests and also use your browser to test a running server.

To validate responses from this function, use the `assert_response` function from `tests.tools`:

```
assert_response(resp, contains=None, matches=None, headers=None, status="200")
```

Pass in the response you get from calling `app.request`, then add things you want checked. Use the `contains` parameter to make sure that the response contains certain values. Use the `status` parameter to check for certain responses. There's actually quite a lot of information in this little function, so it would be good for you to study it.

In the `tests/app_tests.py` automated test I'm first making sure the `/` URL returns a 404 Not Found response, since it actually doesn't exist. Then I'm checking that `/hello` works with both a GET and POST form. Following the test should be fairly simple, even if you might not totally know what's going on.

Take some time studying this latest application, especially how the automated testing works. Make sure you understand how I imported the application from `bin/app.py` and ran it directly for the automated test. This is an important trick that will lead to more learning.

Study Drills

1. Read even more about HTML, and give the simple form a better layout. It helps to draw what you want to do on paper and *then* implement it with HTML.

2. This one is hard, but try to figure out how you'd do a file upload form so that you can upload an image and save it to the disk.

3. This is even more mind-numbing, but go find the HTTP RFC (which is the document that describes how HTTP works) and read as much of it as you can. It is really boring but comes in handy once in a while.

4. This will also be really difficult, but see if you can find someone to help you set up a web server like Apache, Nginx, or thttpd. Try to serve a couple of your .html and .css files with it just to see if you can. Don't worry if you can't. Web servers kind of suck.

5. Take a break after this and just try making as many different web applications as you can. You should *definitely* read about sessions in web.py (which is the same as `lpthw.web`) so you can understand how to keep state for a user.

Common Student Questions

I get `ImportError "No module named bin.app"`.
Again, this is because either you are in the wrong directory, you did not make a `bin/__init__.py` file, or you did not set `PYTHONPATH=.` in your shell. Always remember these solutions, as they are so incredibly common that running to ask why you're getting that error will only slow you down.

I get `__template__() takes no arguments (1 given)` when I run the template.
You probably forgot to put `$def with (greeting)` or a similar variable declaration at the top of the template.

The Start of Your Web Game

We're coming to the end of the book, and in this exercise I'm going to really challenge you. When you're done, you'll be a reasonably competent Python beginner. You'll still need to go through a few more books and write a couple more projects, but you'll have the skills to complete them. The only thing in your way will be time, motivation, and resources.

In this exercise, we won't make a complete game, but instead we'll make an "engine" that can run the game from Exercise 47 in the browser. This will involve refactoring Exercise 43, mixing in the structure from Exercise 47, adding automated tests, and finally creating a web engine that can run the games.

This exercise will be *huge*, and I predict you could spend anywhere from a week to months on it before moving on. It's best to attack it in little chunks and do a bit a night, taking your time to make everything work before moving on.

Refactoring the Exercise 43 Game

You've been altering the gothonweb project for two exercises, and you'll do it one more time in this exercise. The skill you're learning is called "refactoring," or as I like to call it, "fixing stuff." Refactoring is a term programmers use to describe the process of taking old code and changing it to have new features or just to clean it up. You've been doing this without even knowing it, as it's second nature to building software.

What you'll do in this part is take the ideas from Exercise 47 of a testable "map" of rooms and the game from Exercise 43, and combine them together to create a new game structure. It will have the same content, just "refactored" to have a better structure.

The first step is to grab the code from ex47/game.py and copy it to gothonweb/map.py and copy the tests/ex47_tests.py file to tests/map_tests.py and run nosetests again to make sure it keeps working.

NOTE: From now on, I won't show you the output of a test run; just assume that you should be doing it and it'll look like the above unless you have an error.

Once you have the code from Exercise 47 copied over, it's time to refactor it to have the Exercise 43 map in it. I'm going to start off by laying down the basic structure, and then you'll have an assignment to make the map.py file and the map_tests.py file complete.

Lay out the basic structure of the map using the Room class as it is now:

map.py

```
1    class Room(object):
2
3        def __init__(self, name, description):
4            self.name = name
5            self.description = description
6            self.paths = {}
7
8        def go(self, direction):
9            return self.paths.get(direction, None)
10
11        def add_paths(self, paths):
12            self.paths.update(paths)
13
14
15   central_corridor = Room("Central Corridor",
16   """
17   The Gothons of Planet Percal #25 have invaded your ship and destroyed
18   your entire crew.  You are the last surviving member and your last
19   mission is to get the neutron destruct bomb from the Weapons Armory,
20   put it in the bridge, and blow the ship up after getting into an
21   escape pod.
22
23   You're running down the central corridor to the Weapons Armory when
24   a Gothon jumps out, red scaly skin, dark grimy teeth, and evil clown costume
25   flowing around his hate filled body.  He's blocking the door to the
26   Armory and about to pull a weapon to blast you.
27   """)
28
29
30   laser_weapon_armory = Room("Laser Weapon Armory",
31   """
32   Lucky for you they made you learn Gothon insults in the academy.
33   You tell the one Gothon joke you know:
34   Lbhe zbgure vf fb sng, jura fur fvgf nebhaq gur ubhfr, fur fvgf nebhaq gur ubhfr.
35   The Gothon stops, tries not to laugh, then busts out laughing and can't move.
36   While he's laughing you run up and shoot him square in the head
37   putting him down, then jump through the Weapon Armory door.
38
39   You do a dive roll into the Weapon Armory, crouch and scan the room
40   for more Gothons that might be hiding.  It's dead quiet, too quiet.
41   You stand up and run to the far side of the room and find the
42   neutron bomb in its container.  There's a keypad lock on the box
43   and you need the code to get the bomb out.  If you get the code
44   wrong 10 times then the lock closes forever and you can't
45   get the bomb.  The code is 3 digits.
46   """)
47
48
```

```
49    the_bridge = Room("The Bridge",
50    """
51    The container clicks open and the seal breaks, letting gas out.
52    You grab the neutron bomb and run as fast as you can to the
53    bridge where you must place it in the right spot.
54
55    You burst onto the Bridge with the neutron destruct bomb
56    under your arm and surprise 5 Gothons who are trying to
57    take control of the ship.  Each of them has an even uglier
58    clown costume than the last.  They haven't pulled their
59    weapons out yet, as they see the active bomb under your
60    arm and don't want to set it off.
61    """)
62
63
64    escape_pod = Room("Escape Pod",
65    """
66    You point your blaster at the bomb under your arm
67    and the Gothons put their hands up and start to sweat.
68    You inch backward to the door, open it, and then carefully
69    place the bomb on the floor, pointing your blaster at it.
70    You then jump back through the door, punch the close button
71    and blast the lock so the Gothons can't get out.
72    Now that the bomb is placed you run to the escape pod to
73    get off this tin can.
74
75    You rush through the ship desperately trying to make it to
76    the escape pod before the whole ship explodes.  It seems like
77    hardly any Gothons are on the ship, so your run is clear of
78    interference.  You get to the chamber with the escape pods, and
79    now need to pick one to take.  Some of them could be damaged
80    but you don't have time to look.  There's 5 pods, which one
81    do you take?
82    """)
83
84
85    the_end_winner = Room("The End",
86    """
87    You jump into pod 2 and hit the eject button.
88    The pod easily slides out into space heading to
89    the planet below.  As it flies to the planet, you look
90    back and see your ship implode then explode like a
91    bright star, taking out the Gothon ship at the same
92    time.  You won!
93    """)
94
95
96    the_end_loser = Room("The End",
97    """
98    You jump into a random pod and hit the eject button.
99    The pod escapes out into the void of space, then
```

```
100    implodes as the hull ruptures, crushing your body
101    into jam jelly.
102    """
103    )
104
105    escape_pod.add_paths({
106        '2': the_end_winner,
107        '*': the_end_loser
108    })
109
110    generic_death = Room("death", "You died.")
111
112    the_bridge.add_paths({
113        'throw the bomb': generic_death,
114        'slowly place the bomb': escape_pod
115    })
116
117    laser_weapon_armory.add_paths({
118        '0132': the_bridge,
119        '*': generic_death
120    })
121
122    central_corridor.add_paths({
123        'shoot!': generic_death,
124        'dodge!': generic_death,
125        'tell a joke': laser_weapon_armory
126    })
127
128    START = central_corridor
```

You'll notice that there are a couple of problems with our Room class and this map:

1. We have to put the text that was in the if-else clauses that got printed *before* entering a room as part of each room. This means you can't shuffle the map around, which would be nice. You'll be fixing that up in this exercise.

2. There are parts in the original game where we ran code that determined things like the bomb's keypad code, or the right pod. In this game, we just pick some defaults and go with it, but later you'll be given Study Drills to make this work again.

3. I've just made a generic_death ending for all the bad decisions, which you'll have to finish for me. You'll need to go back through and add in all the original endings and make sure they work.

4. I've got a new kind of transition labeled "*" that will be used for a "catch-all" action in the engine.

Once you've got that basically written out, here's the new automated test tests/map_test.py that you should have to get yourself started:

```
1    from nose.tools import *
2    from gothonweb.map import *
3
4    def test_room():
5        gold = Room("GoldRoom",
6                    """This room has gold in it you can grab. There's a
7                    door to the north.""")
8        assert_equal(gold.name, "GoldRoom")
9        assert_equal(gold.paths, [])
10
11   def test_room_paths():
12       center = Room("Center", "Test room in the center.")
13       north = Room("North", "Test room in the north.")
14       south = Room("South", "Test room in the south.")
15
16       center.add_paths(['north': north, 'south': south])
17       assert_equal(center.go('north'), north)
18       assert_equal(center.go('south'), south)
19
20   def test_map():
21       start = Room("Start", "You can go west and down a hole.")
22       west = Room("Trees", "There are trees here, you can go east.")
23       down = Room("Dungeon", "It's dark down here, you can go up.")
24
25       start.add_paths(['west': west, 'down': down])
26       west.add_paths(['east': start])
27       down.add_paths(['up': start])
28
29       assert_equal(start.go('west'), west)
30       assert_equal(start.go('west').go('east'), start)
31       assert_equal(start.go('down').go('up'), start)
32
33   def test_gothon_game_map():
34       assert_equal(START.go('shoot!'), generic_death)
35       assert_equal(START.go('dodge!'), generic_death)
36
37       room = START.go('tell a joke')
38       assert_equal(room, laser_weapon_armory)
```

Your task in this part of the exercise is to complete the map, and make the automated test completely validate the whole map. This includes fixing all the generic_death objects to be real endings. Make sure this works really well and that your test is as complete as possible, because we'll be changing this map later and you'll use the tests to make sure it keeps working.

Sessions and Tracking Users

At a certain point in your web application, you'll need to keep track of some information and associate it with the user's browser. The web (because of HTTP) is what we like to call "stateless," which means each request you make is independent of any other requests being made. If you request page A, put in some data, and click a link to page B, all the data you sent to page A just disappears.

The solution to this is to create a little data store (usually in a database or on the disk) that uses a number unique to each browser to keep track of what that browser was doing. In the little lpthw.web framework, it's fairly easy. Here's an example showing how it's done:

session_sample.py

```
1    import web
2
3    web.config.debug = False
4
5    urls = (
6        "/count", "count",
7        "/reset", "reset"
8    )
9    app = web.application(urls, locals())
10   store = web.session.DiskStore('sessions')
11   session = web.session.Session(app, store, initializer={'count': 0})
12
13   class count:
14       def GET(self):
15           session.count += 1
16           return str(session.count)
17
18   class reset:
19       def GET(self):
20           session.kill()
21           return ""
22
23   if __name__ == "__main__":
24       app.run()
```

To make this work, you need to create a sessions/ directory where the application can put session storage. Do that, run this application, and go to /count. Hit refresh and watch the counter go up. Close the browser and it *forgets* who you are, which is what we want for the game. There's a way to make the browser remember forever, but that makes testing and development harder. If you then go to /reset and back to /count, you can see your counter reset because you've killed the session.

Take the time to understand this code so you can see how the session starts off with the count equal to 0. Also try looking at the files in sessions/ to see if you can open them up. Here's a Python session where I open up one and decode it:

```
>>> import pickle
>>> import base64
>>> base64.b64decode(open("sessions/XXXXX").read())
"(dp1\nS'count'\np2\nI1\nsS'ip'\np3\nV127.0.0.1\np4\nsS'session_id'\np5\nS'XXXX'\np6\ns."
>>>
>>> x = base64.b64decode(open("sessions/XXXXX").read())
>>>
>>> pickle.loads(x)
{'count': 1, 'ip': u'127.0.0.1', 'session_id': 'XXXXX'}
```

The sessions are really just dictionaries that get written to disk using `pickle` and `base64` libraries. There are probably as many ways to store and manage sessions as there are web frameworks, so it's not too important to know how these work. It does help if you need to debug the session or potentially clean it out.

Creating an Engine

You should have your game map working and a good unit test for it. I now want you to make a simple little game engine that will run the rooms, collect input from the player, and keep track of where a play is in the game. We'll be using the sessions you just learned to make a simple game engine that will:

1. Start a new game for new users.

2. Present the room to the user.

3. Take input from the user.

4. Run user input through the game.

5. Display the results and keep going until the user dies.

To do this, you're going to take the trusty `bin/app.py` you've been hacking on and create a fully working, session-based game engine. The catch is I'm going to make a very simple one with *basic HTML* files, and it'll be up to you to complete it. Here's the base engine:

app.py

```
1    import web
2    from gothonweb import map
3
4    urls = (
5      '/game', 'GameEngine',
6      '/', 'Index',
7    )
8
9    app = web.application(urls, globals())
10
```

```
11    # little hack so that debug mode works with sessions
12    if web.config.get('_session') is None:
13        store = web.session.DiskStore('sessions')
14        session = web.session.Session(app, store,
15                                      initializer={'room': None})
16        web.config._session = session
17    else:
18        session = web.config._session
19
20    render = web.template.render('templates/', base="layout")
21
22
23    class Index(object):
24        def GET(self):
25            # this is used to "setup" the session with starting values
26            session.room = map.START
27            web.seeother("/game")
28
29
30    class GameEngine(object):
31
32        def GET(self):
33            if session.room:
34                return render.show_room(room=session.room)
35            else:
36                # why is there here? do you need it?
37                return render.you_died()
38
39        def POST(self):
40            form = web.input(action=None)
41
42            # there is a bug here, can you fix it?
43            if session.room and form.action:
44                session.room = session.room.go(form.action)
45
46            web.seeother("/game")
47
48    if __name__ == "__main__":
49        app.run()
```

There are even more new things in this script, but amazingly it's an entire web-based game engine in a small file. The biggest "hack" in the script are the lines that bring the sessions back, which is needed so that debug mode reloading works. Otherwise, each time you hit refresh, the sessions will disappear and the game won't work.

Before you run bin/app.py you need to change your PYTHONPATH environment variable. Don't know what that is? I know, it's kind of dumb that you have to learn what this is to run even basic Python programs, but that's how Python people like things.

In your Terminal, type:

```
export PYTHONPATH=$PYTHONPATH:.
```

On Windows PowerShell, type:

```
$env:PYTHONPATH = "$env:PYTHONPATH;."
```

You should only have to do it once per shell session, but if you get an import error, then you probably need to do this or you did it wrong.

You should next delete `templates/hello_form.html` and `templates/index.html` and create the two templates mentioned in the above code. Here's a *very* simple `templates/show_room.html`:

show_room.html

```
$def with (room)

<h1> $room.name </h1>

<pre>
$room.description
</pre>

$if room.name == "death":
    <p><a href="/">Play Again?</a></p>
$else:
    <p>
    <form action="/game" method="POST">
        - <input type="text" name="action"> <input type="SUBMIT">
    </form>
    </p>
```

That is the template to show a room as you travel through the game. Next you need one to tell users they died in the case that they got to the end of the map on accident, which is `templates/you_died.html`:

you_died.html

```
<h1>You Died!</h1>

<p>Looks like you bit the dust.</p>
<p><a href="/">Play Again</a></p>
```

With those in place, you should now be able to do the following:

1.   Get the test `tests/app_tests.py` working again so that you are testing the game. You won't be able to do much more than a few clicks in the game because of sessions, but you should be able to do some basics.

2.   Remove the `sessions/*` files and make sure you've started over.

3.   Run the `python bin/app.py` script and test out the game.

You should be able to refresh and fix the game like normal and work with the game HTML and engine until it does all the things you want it to do.

Your Final Exam

Do you feel like this was a huge amount of information thrown at you all at once? Good, I want you to have something to tinker with while you build your skills. To complete this exercise, I'm going to give you a final set of exercises for you to complete on your own. You'll notice that what you've written so far isn't very well built; it is just a first version of the code. Your task now is to make the game more complete by doing these things:

1.   Fix all the bugs I mention in the code, as well as any that I didn't mention. If you find new bugs, let me know.

2.   Improve all the automated tests so that you test more of the application and get to a point where you use a test rather than your browser to check the application while you work.

3.   Make the HTML look better.

4.   Research logins and create a signup system for the application, so people can have logins and high scores.

5.   Complete the game map, making it as large and feature-complete as possible.

6.   Give people a "help" system that lets them ask what they can do at each room in the game.

7.   Add any other features you can think of to the game.

8.   Create several "maps" and let people choose a game they want to run. Your `bin/app.py` engine should be able to run any map of rooms you give it, so you can support multiple games.

9.   Finally, use what you learned in Exercises 48 and 49 to create a better input processor. You have most of the code necessary; you just need to improve the grammar and hook it up to your input form and the `GameEngine`.

Good luck!

Common Student Questions

I'm using `sessions` in my game and I can't test it with `nosetests`.
You need to read about sessions in the reloader: http://webpy.org/cookbook/session_with_reloader.

I get an `ImportError`.
Wrong directory. Wrong Python version. PYTHONPATH not set. No `__init__.py` file. Spelling mistake in import.

Next Steps

You're not a programmer quite yet. I like to think of this book as giving you your "programming black belt." You know enough to start another book on programming and handle it just fine. This book should have given you the mental tools and attitude you need to go through most Python books and actually learn something. It might even make it easy.

I recommend you check out some of these projects and try to build something with them:

- The Django Tutorial (https://docs.djangoproject.com/en/1.4/intro/tutorial01) and try to build a web application with the Django Web Framework (https://www.djangoproject.com).

- SciPy (http://www.scipy.org), if you're into science, math, and engineering and also Dexy (http://dexy.it), for when you want to write awesome papers that incorporate SciPy or any code really.

- PyGame (http://www.pygame.org/news.html) and see if you can make a game with graphics and sound.

- Pandas (http://pandas.pydata.org) for doing data manipulation and analysis.

- Natural Language Tool Kit (http://nltk.org) for analyzing written text and writing things like spam filters and chat bots.

- Requests (http://docs.python-requests.org/en/latest/index.html) to learn the client side of HTTP and the web.

- SimpleCV (http://simplecv.org) to play with making your computer see things in the real world.

- ScraPy (http://scrapy.org) and try scraping some websites to get information off them.

- Panda3D (https://www.panda3d.org) for doing 3D graphic and games.

- Kivy (http://kivy.org) for doing user interfaces on desktops and mobile platforms.

- SciKit-Learn (http://scikit-learn.org/stable) for machine learning applications.

- Ren'Py (http://renpy.org) for doing interactive fiction games, similar to what you've built in this book but with pictures.

- Learn C the Hard Way (http://c.learncodethehardway.org) after you're familiar with Python and try learning C and algorithms with my other book. Take it slow; C is different but a very good thing to learn.

Pick one of the above projects, and go through any tutorials and documentation they have. As you go through it, *type in all the code* and make it work. That's how I do it. That's how every programmer does it. Reading programming documentation is not enough to learn it; you have to do it. After you get through the tutorial and any other documentation they have, make something. Anything will do, even something someone else has already written. Just make something.

Just understand anything you write will probably suck. That's alright though; I suck at every programming language I first start using. Nobody writes pure perfect gold when they're a beginner, and anyone who tells you they did is a huge liar.

How to Learn Any Programming Language

I'm going to teach you how to learn most of the programming languages you may want to learn in the future. The organization of this book is based on how I and many other programmers learn new languages. Here's the process that I usually follow:

1.   Get a book or some introductory text about the language.

2.   Go through the book and type in all the code, making it run.

3.   Read the book as you work on the code, taking notes.

4.   Use the language to implement a small set of programs you are familiar with in another language.

5.   Read other people's code in the language, and try to copy their patterns.

In this book, I forced you to go through this process very slowly and in small chunks. Other books aren't organized the same way and this means you have to extrapolate how I've made you do this to how their content is organized. Best way to do this is to read the book lightly and make a list of all the major code sections. Turn this list into a set of exercises based on the chapters and then simply do them in order, one at a time.

The above process also works for new technologies, assuming they have books you can read. For anything without books, you do the above process but use online documentation or source code as your initial introduction.

Each new language you learn makes you a better programmer, and as you learn more, they become easier to learn. By your third or fourth language, you should be able to pick up similar languages in a week, with stranger languages taking longer. Now that you know Python, you could potentially learn Ruby and JavaScript fairly quickly by comparison. This is simply because many languages share similar concepts, and once you learn the concepts in one language, they work in others.

The final thing to remember about learning a new language: don't be a stupid tourist. A stupid tourist is someone who goes to another country and then complains that the food isn't like the food at home. "Why can't I get a good burger in this stupid country!?" When you're learning a new language, assume that what it does isn't stupid—it's just different—and embrace it so you can learn it.

After you learn a language though, don't be a slave to that language's way of doing things. Sometimes the people who use a language actually do some very idiotic things for no other reason than "that's how we've always done it." If you like your style better and you know how everyone else does it, then feel free to break their rules if it improves things.

I personally really enjoy learning new programming languages. I think of myself as a "programmer anthropologist" and think of them as little insights about the group of programmers who use them. I'm learning a language they all use to talk to each other through computers, and I find this fascinating. Then again I'm kind of a weird guy, so just learn programming languages because you want to.

Enjoy! This is really fun stuff.

Advice from an Old Programmer

You've finished this book and have decided to continue with programming. Maybe it will be a career for you, or maybe it will be a hobby. You'll need some advice to make sure you continue on the right path and get the most enjoyment out of your newly chosen activity.

I've been programming for a very long time. So long that it's incredibly boring to me. At the time that I wrote this book, I knew about 20 programming languages and could learn new ones in about a day to a week, depending on how weird they were. Eventually, though, this just became boring and couldn't hold my interest anymore. This doesn't mean I think programming *is* boring, or that *you* will think it's boring, only that *I* find it uninteresting at this point in my journey.

What I discovered after this journey of learning is that it's not the languages that matter but what you do with them. Actually, I always knew that, but I'd get distracted by the languages and forget it periodically. Now I never forget it, and neither should you.

Which programming language you learn and use doesn't matter. Do *not* get sucked into the religion surrounding programming languages, as that will only blind you to their true purpose of being your tool for doing interesting things.

Programming as an intellectual activity is the *only* art form that allows you to create interactive art. You can create projects that other people can play with, and you can talk to them indirectly. No other art form is quite this interactive. Movies flow to the audience in one direction. Paintings do not move. Code goes both ways.

Programming as a profession is only moderately interesting. It can be a good job, but you could make about the same money and be happier running a fast food joint. You're much better off using code as your secret weapon in another profession.

People who can code in the world of technology companies are a dime a dozen and get no respect. People who can code in biology, medicine, government, sociology, physics, history, and mathematics are respected and can do amazing things to advance those disciplines.

Of course, all this advice is pointless. If you liked learning to write software with this book, you should try to use it to improve your life any way you can. Go out and explore this weird, wonderful, new intellectual pursuit that barely anyone in the last 50 years has been able to explore. Might as well enjoy it while you can.

Finally, I'll say that learning to create software changes you and makes you different—not better or worse, just different. You may find that people treat you harshly because you can create software, maybe using words like "nerd." Maybe you'll find that because you can dissect their logic, they hate arguing with you. You may even find that simply knowing how a computer works makes you annoying and weird to them.

To this, I have just one piece of advice: they can go to hell. The world needs more weird people who know how things work and who love to figure it all out. When they treat you like this, just remember that this is *your* journey, not theirs. Being different is not a crime, and people who tell you it is are just jealous that you've picked up a skill they never in their wildest dreams could acquire.

You can code. They cannot. That is pretty damn cool.

Command Line Crash Course

This appendix is a super fast course in using the command line. It is intended to be done rapidly in about a day or two and not meant to teach you advanced shell usage.

Introduction: Shut Up and Shell

This appendix is a crash course in using the command line to make your computer perform tasks. As a crash course, it's not as detailed or extensive as my other books. It is simply designed to get you barely capable enough to start using your computer like a real programmer does. When you're done with this appendix, you will be able to give most of the basic commands that every shell user touches every day. You'll understand the basics of directories and a few other concepts.

The only piece of advice I am going to give you is this:

Shut up and type all this in.

Sorry to be mean, but that's what you have to do. If you have an irrational fear of the command line, the only way to conquer an irrational fear is to just shut up and fight through it.

You are not going to destroy your computer. You are not going to be thrown into some jail at the bottom of Microsoft's Redmond campus. Your friends won't laugh at you for being a nerd. Simply ignore any stupid weird reasons you have for fearing the command line.

Why? Because if you want to learn to code, then you must learn this. Programming languages are advanced ways to control your computer with language. The command line is the little baby brother of programming languages. Learning the command line teaches you to control the computer using language. Once you get past that, you can then move on to writing code and feeling like you actually own the hunk of metal you just bought.

How to Use This Appendix

The best way to use this appendix is to do the following:

- Get yourself a small paper notebook and a pen.
- Start at the beginning of the appendix and do each exercise exactly as you're told.

- When you read something that doesn't make sense or that you don't understand, *write it down in your notebook*. Leave a little space so you can write an answer.

- After you finish an exercise, go back through your notebook and review the questions you have. Try to answer them by searching online and asking friends who might know the answer. Email me at help@learncodethehardway.org and I'll help you too.

Just keep going through this process of doing an exercise, writing down questions you have, then going back through and answering the questions you can. By the time you're done, you'll actually know a lot more than you think about using the command line.

You Will Be Memorizing Things

I'm warning you ahead of time that I'm going to make you memorize things right away. This is the quickest way to get you capable at something, but for some people, memorization is painful. Just fight through it and do it anyway. Memorization is an important skill in learning things, so you should get over your fear of it.

Here's how you memorize things:

- Tell yourself you *will* do it. Don't try to find tricks or easy ways out of it; just sit down and do it.

- Write what you want to memorize on some index cards. Put one half of what you need to learn on one side, then another half on the other side.

- Every day for about 15–30 minutes, drill yourself on the index cards, trying to recall each one. Put any cards you don't get right into a different pile; just drill those cards until you get bored, then try the whole deck and see if you improve.

- Before you go to bed, drill just the cards you got wrong for about 5 minutes, then go to sleep.

There are other techniques, like you can write what you need to learn on a sheet of paper, laminate it, then stick it to the wall of your shower. While you're bathing, drill the knowledge without looking, and when you get stuck glance at it to refresh your memory.

If you do this every day, you should be able to memorize most things I tell you to memorize in about a week to a month. Once you do, nearly everything else becomes easier and intuitive, which is the purpose of memorization. It's not to teach you abstract concepts, but rather to ingrain the basics so that they are intuitive and you don't have to think about them. Once you've memorized these basics, they stop being speed bumps, preventing you from learning more advanced abstract concepts.

Exercise 1: The Setup

In this appendix, you will be instructed to do three things:

- Do some things in your shell (command line, Terminal, PowerShell).

- Learn about what you just did.

- Do more on your own.

For this first exercise, you'll be expected to get your Terminal open and working so that you can do the rest of the appendix.

Do This

Get your Terminal, shell, or PowerShell working so you can access it quickly and know that it works.

Mac OSX

For Mac OSX, you'll need to do this:

- Hold down the command key and hit the spacebar.

- In the top right the blue "search bar" will pop up.

- Type "terminal."

- Click on the Terminal application that looks kind of like a black box.

- This will open Terminal.

- You can now go to your dock and CTRL-click to pull up the menu, then select `Options->Keep in dock`.

Now you have your Terminal open, and it's in your dock so you can get to it.

Linux

I'm assuming that if you have Linux, then you already know how to get at your Terminal. Look through the menu for your window manager for anything named "Shell" or "Terminal."

Windows

On Windows we're going to use PowerShell. People used to work with a program called cmd.exe, but it's not nearly as usable as PowerShell. If you have Windows 7 or later, do this:

- Click Start.

- In "Search programs and files," type "powershell."

- Hit Enter.

If you don't have Windows 7, you should *seriously* consider upgrading. If you still insist on not upgrading, then you can try installing it from Microsoft's download center. Search online to find "powershell downloads" for your version of Windows. You are on your own, though, since I don't have Windows XP, but hopefully the PowerShell experience is the same.

You Learned This

You learned how to get your Terminal open, so you can do the rest of this appendix.

NOTE: If you have that really smart friend who already knows Linux, ignore him when he tells you to use something other than Bash. I'm teaching you Bash. That's it. He will claim that zsh will give you 30 more IQ points and win you millions in the stock market. Ignore him. Your goal is to get capable enough, and at this level, it doesn't matter which shell you use. The next warning is stay off IRC or other places where "hackers" hang out. They think it's funny to hand you commands that can destroy your computer. The command rm -rf / is a classic that you *must never type*. Just avoid them. If you need help, make sure you get it from someone you trust and not from random idiots on the internet.

Do More

This exercise has a large "do more" part. The other exercises are not as involved as this one, but I'm having you prime your brain for the rest of the appendix by doing some memorization. Just trust me: this will make things silky smooth later on.

Linux/Mac OSX

Take this list of commands and create index cards with the names on the left on one side and the definitions on the other side. Drill them every day while continuing with the lessons in this appendix.

pwd   print working directory

hostname   my computer's network name

mkdir   make directory

cd   change directory

ls   list directory

rmdir   remove directory

pushd   push directory

popd   pop directory

cp   copy a file or directory

mv   move a file or directory

less   page through a file

cat   print the whole file

xargs   execute arguments

find   find files

grep   find things inside files

man   read a manual page

apropos   find what man page is appropriate

env   look at your environment

echo   print some arguments

export   export/set a new environment variable

exit   exit the shell

sudo   DANGER! become super user root DANGER!

Windows

If you're using Windows, then here's your list of commands:

pwd   print working directory

hostname   my computer's network name

mkdir   make directory

cd   change directory

ls   list directory

rmdir   remove directory

pushd   push directory

popd   pop directory

cp   copy a file or directory

robocopy   robust copy

mv   move a file or directory

more   page through a file

type   print the whole file

forfiles   run a command on lots of files

dir -r   find files

select-string   find things inside files

help   read a manual page

helpctr   find what man page is appropriate

echo   print some arguments

set   export/set a new environment variable

exit   exit the shell

runas   DANGER! become super user root DANGER!

Drill, drill, drill! Drill until you can say these phrases right away when you see that word. Then drill the inverse, so that you read the phrase and know what command will do that. You're building your vocabulary by doing this, but don't spend so much time you go nuts and get bored.

Exercise 2: Paths, Folders, Directories (pwd)

In this exercise, you learn how to print your working directory with the pwd command.

Do This

I'm going to teach you how to read these "sessions" that I show you. You don't have to type everything I list here, just some of the parts:

- You do *not* type in the $ (Unix) or ^gt; (Windows). That's just me showing you my session so you can see what I got.

- You type in the stuff after $ or >, then hit Enter. So if I have $ pwd you type just pwd and hit Enter.

- You can then see what I have for output followed by another $ or > prompt. That content is the output, and you should see the same output.

Let's do a simple first command so you can get the hang of this:

Exercise 2 Session

```
$ pwd
/Users/zedshaw
$
```

```
PS C:\Users\zed> pwd

Path
----
C:\Users\zed

PS C:\Users\zed>
```

NOTE: In this appendix, I need to save space so that you can focus on the important details of the commands. To do this, I'm going to strip out the first part of the prompt (the PS C:\Users\zed above) and leave just the little > part. This means your prompt won't look exactly the same, but don't worry about that. Remember that from now on I'll only have the > to tell you that's the prompt. I'm doing the same thing for the Unix prompts, but Unix prompts are so varied that most people get used to $ meaning "just the prompt."

You Learned This

Your prompt will look different from mine. You may have your user name before the $ and the name of your computer. On Windows it will probably look different too. The key is that you see the following pattern:

- There's a prompt.

- You type a command there. In this case, it's pwd.

- It printed something.

- Repeat.

You just learned what pwd does, which means "print working directory." What's a directory? It's a folder. "Folder" and "directory" mean the same thing, and they're used interchangeably. When you open your file browser on your computer to graphically find files, you are walking through folders. Those folders are the exact same things as these "directories" we're going to work with.

Do More

- Type pwd 20 times and each time say, "print working directory."

- Write down the path that this command gives you. Find it with your graphical file browser of choice.

- No, seriously, type it 20 times and say it out loud. Shhh. Just do it.

Exercise 3: If You Get Lost

As you go through these instructions, you may get lost. You may not know where you are or where a file is and have no idea how to continue. To solve this problem, I am going to teach you the commands to type to stop being lost.

Whenever you get lost, it is most likely because you were typing commands and have no idea where you've ended up. What you should do is type pwd to *print your current directory*. This tells you where you are.

The next thing is you need to have a way of getting back to where you are safe, your home. To do this, type cd ~ and you are back in your home.

This means if you get lost at any time, type:

```
pwd
cd ~
```

The first command pwd tells you where you are. The second command cd ~ takes you home so you can try again.

Do This

Right now, figure out where you are, and then go home using pwd and cd ~. This will make sure you are always in the right place.

You Learned This

How to get back to your home if you ever get lost.

Exercise 4: Make a Directory (mkdir)

In this exercise, you learn how to make a new directory (folder) using the mkdir command.

Do This

Remember! *You need to go home first!* Do your pwd then cd ~ before doing this exercise. Before you do *all* exercises in this appendix, always go home first!

Exercise 4 Session

```
$ pwd
$ cd ~
```

```
$ mkdir temp
$ mkdir temp/stuff
$ mkdir temp/stuff/things
$ mkdir -p temp/stuff/things/frank/joe/alex/john
$
```

```
> pwd
> cd ~
> mkdir temp
```

    Directory: C:\Users\zed

Mode   LastWriteTime   Length Name
----   -------------   ------ ----
d----   12/17/2011   9:02 AM   temp


```
> mkdir temp/stuff
```

    Directory: C:\Users\zed\temp

Mode   LastWriteTime   Length Name
----   -------------   ------ ----
d----   12/17/2011   9:02 AM   stuff


```
> mkdir temp/stuff/things
```

    Directory: C:\Users\zed\temp\stuff

Mode   LastWriteTime   Length Name
----   -------------   ------ ----
d----   12/17/2011   9:03 AM   things


```
> mkdir temp/stuff/things/frank/joe/alex/john
```

    Directory: C:\Users\zed\temp\stuff\things\frank\joe\alex

Mode   LastWriteTime   Length Name
----   -------------   ------ ----
d----   12/17/2011   9:03 AM   john


```
>
```

This is the only time I'll list the pwd and cd ~ commands. They are expected in the exercises *every time*. Do them all the time.

You Learned This

Now we get into typing more than one command. These are all the different ways you can run mkdir. What does mkdir do? It make directories. Why are you asking that? You should be doing your index cards and getting your commands memorized. If you don't know that "mkdir makes directories," then keep working the index cards.

What does it mean to make a directory? You might call directories "folders." They're the same thing. All you did above is create directories inside directories inside of more directories. This is called a "path," and it's a way of saying, "first temp, then stuff, then things and that's where I want it." It's a set of directions to the computer of where you want to put something in the tree of folders (directories) that make up your computer's hard disk.

NOTE: In this appendix, I'm using the / (slash) character for all paths, since they work the same on all computers now. However, Windows users will need to know that you can also use the \ (backslash) character. Other Windows users may expect to see the backslash at all times, but this isn't necessary.

Do More

- The concept of a "path" might confuse you at this point. Don't worry. We'll do a lot more with them and then you'll get it.

- Make 20 other directories inside the temp directory in various levels. Go look at them with a graphical file browser.

- Make a directory with a space in the name by putting quotes around it: mkdir "I Have Fun".

- If the temp directory already exists, then you'll get an error. Use cd to change to a work directory that you can control and try it there. On Windows, the desktop is a good place.

Exercise 5: Change Directory (cd)

In this exercise, you learn how to change from one directory to another using the cd command.

Do This

I'm going to give you the instructions for these sessions one more time:

- You do *not* type in the $ (Unix) or > (Windows).

- You type in the stuff after this, then hit Enter. If I have $ cd temp, you just type cd temp and hit Enter.

- The output comes after you hit Enter, followed by another $ or > prompt.

- Always go home first! Do pwd and then cd ~ so you go back to your starting point.

Exercise 5 Session

```
$ cd temp
$ pwd
~/temp
$ cd stuff
$ pwd
~/temp/stuff
$ cd things
$ pwd
~/temp/stuff/things
$ cd frank/
$ pwd
~/temp/stuff/things/frank
$ cd joe/
$ pwd
~/temp/stuff/things/frank/joe
$ cd alex/
$ pwd
~/temp/stuff/things/frank/joe/alex
$ cd john/
$ pwd
~/temp/stuff/things/frank/joe/alex/john
$ cd ..
$ cd ..
$ pwd
~/temp/stuff/things/frank/joe
$ cd ..
$ cd ..
$ pwd
~/temp/stuff/things
$ cd ../../..
$ pwd
~/
$ cd temp/stuff/things/frank/joe/alex/john
$ pwd
~/temp/stuff/things/frank/joe/alex/john
$ cd ../../../../../../../
$ pwd
~/
$
```

Exercise 5 Windows Session

```
> cd temp
> pwd
```

```
Path
----
C:\Users\zed\temp


> cd stuff
> pwd

Path
----
C:\Users\zed\temp\stuff


> cd things
> pwd

Path
----
C:\Users\zed\temp\stuff\things


> cd frank
> pwd

Path
----
C:\Users\zed\temp\stuff\things\frank


> cd joe
> pwd

Path
----
C:\Users\zed\temp\stuff\things\frank\joe


> cd alex
> pwd

Path
----
C:\Users\zed\temp\stuff\things\frank\joe\alex


> cd john
> pwd

Path
----
C:\Users\zed\temp\stuff\things\frank\joe\alex\john
```

```
> cd ..
> cd ..
> cd ..
> pwd

Path
----
C:\Users\zed\temp\stuff\things\frank


> cd ../..
> pwd

Path
----
C:\Users\zed\temp\stuff


> cd ..
> cd ..
> cd temp/stuff/things/frank/joe/alex/john
> cd ../../../../../../../
> pwd

Path
----
C:\Users\zed


>
```

You Learned This

You made all these directories in the last exercise, and now you're just moving around inside them with the cd command. In my session above, I also use pwd to check where I am, so remember not to type the output that pwd prints. For example, on line 3, you see ~/temp, but that's the output of pwd from the prompt above it. *Do not type this in.*

You should also see how I use the .. to move "up" in the tree and path.

Do More

A very important part of learning to use the command line interface (CLI) on a computer with a graphical user interface (GUI) is figuring out how they work together. When I started using computers, there was no "GUI" and you did everything with the DOS prompt (the CLI). Later, when computers became powerful enough that everyone could have graphics, it was simple for me to match CLI directories with GUI windows and folders.

Most people today, however, have no comprehension of the CLI, paths, and directories. In fact, it's very difficult to teach it to them, and the only way to learn about the connection is for you to constantly work with the CLI, until one day it clicks that things you do in the GUI will show up in the CLI.

The way you do this is by spending some time finding directories with your GUI file browser, then going to them with your CLI. This is what you'll do next:

- cd to the joe directory with one command.

- cd back to temp with one command, but not further above that.

- Find out how to cd to your "home directory" with one command.

- cd to your Documents directory, then find it with your GUI file browser (Finder, Windows Explorer, etc.).

- cd to your Downloads directory, then find it with your file browser.

- Find another directory with your file browser, then cd to it.

- Remember when you put quotes around a directory with spaces in it? You can do that with any command. For example, if you have a directory I Have Fun, then you can do cd "I Have Fun".

Exercise 6: List Directory (ls)

In this exercise, you learn how to list the contents of a directory with the ls command.

Do This

Before you start, make sure you cd back to the directory above temp. If you have no idea where you are, use pwd to figure it out and then move there.

Exercise 6 Session

```
$ cd temp
$ ls
stuff
$ cd stuff
$ ls
things
$ cd things
$ ls
frank
$ cd frank
$ ls
joe
```

```
$ cd joe
$ ls
alex
$ cd alex
$ ls
$ cd john
$ ls
$ cd ..
$ ls
john
$ cd ../../../
$ ls
frank
$ cd ../../
$ ls
stuff
$
```

```
> cd temp
> ls
```

    Directory: C:\Users\zed\temp

Mode   LastWriteTime   Length Name
----   -------------   ------ ----
d----   12/17/2011   9:03 AM   stuff

```
> cd stuff
> ls
```

    Directory: C:\Users\zed\temp\stuff

Mode   LastWriteTime   Length Name
----   -------------   ------ ----
d----   12/17/2011   9:03 AM   things

```
> cd things
> ls
```

    Directory: C:\Users\zed\temp\stuff\things

Mode   LastWriteTime   Length Name
----   -------------   ------ ----

```
d----          12/17/2011   9:03 AM                frank


> cd frank
> ls


    Directory: C:\Users\zed\temp\stuff\things\frank


Mode                LastWriteTime        Length Name
----                -------------        ------ ----
d----          12/17/2011   9:03 AM                joe


> cd joe
> ls


    Directory: C:\Users\zed\temp\stuff\things\frank\joe


Mode                LastWriteTime        Length Name
----                -------------        ------ ----
d----          12/17/2011   9:03 AM                alex


> cd alex
> ls


    Directory: C:\Users\zed\temp\stuff\things\frank\joe\alex


Mode                LastWriteTime        Length Name
----                -------------        ------ ----
d----          12/17/2011   9:03 AM                john


> cd john
> ls
> cd ..
> ls


    Directory: C:\Users\zed\temp\stuff\things\frank\joe\alex


Mode                LastWriteTime        Length Name
----                -------------        ------ ----
d----          12/17/2011   9:03 AM                john
```

```
> cd ..
> ls
```

        Directory: C:\Users\zed\temp\stuff\things\frank\joe

Mode   LastWriteTime   Length Name
----   -------------   ------ ----
d----   12/17/2011   9:03 AM   alex

```
> cd ../../..
> ls
```

        Directory: C:\Users\zed\temp\stuff

Mode   LastWriteTime   Length Name
----   -------------   ------ ----
d----   12/17/2011   9:03 AM   things

```
> cd ..
> ls
```

        Directory: C:\Users\zed\temp

Mode   LastWriteTime   Length Name
----   -------------   ------ ----
d----   12/17/2011   9:03 AM   stuff

```
>
```

You Learned This

The ls command lists out the contents of the directory you are currently in. You can see me use cd to change into different directories and then list what's in them so I know which directory to go to next.

There are a lot of options for the ls command, but you'll learn how to get help on those later when we cover the help command.

Do More

- *Type every one of these commands in!* You have to actually type these to learn them. Just reading them is *not* good enough. I'll stop yelling now.

- On Unix, try the `ls -lR` command while you're in `temp`.

- On Windows do the same thing with `dir -R`.

- Use `cd` to get to other directories on your computer and then use `ls` to see what's in them.

- Update your notebook with new questions. I know you probably have some, because I'm not covering everything about this command.

- Remember that if you get lost, then use `ls` and pwd to figure out where you are, then go to where you need to be with `cd`.

Exercise 7: Remove Directory (rmdir)

In this exercise, you learn how to remove an empty directory.

Do This

Exercise 7 Session

```
$ cd temp
$ ls
stuff
$ cd stuff/things/frank/joe/alex/john/
$ cd ..
$ rmdir john
$ cd ..
$ rmdir alex
$ cd ..
$ ls
joe
$ rmdir joe
$ cd ..
$ ls
frank
$ rmdir frank
$ cd ..
$ ls
things
$ rmdir things
$ cd ..
$ ls
```

```
stuff
$ rmdir stuff
$ pwd
~/temp
$
```

WARNING! If you try to do rmdir on Mac OSX and it refuses to remove the directory even though you are *positive* it's empty, then there is actually a file in there called .DS_Store. In that case, type rm -rf <dir> instead (replace <dir> with the directory name).

Exercise 7 Windows Session

```
> cd temp
> ls


    Directory: C:\Users\zed\temp


Mode                LastWriteTime     Length Name
----                -------------     ------ ----
d----         12/17/2011    9:03 AM          stuff


> cd stuff/things/frank/joe/alex/john/
> cd ..
> rmdir john
> cd ..
> rmdir alex
> cd ..
> rmdir joe
> cd ..
> rmdir frank
> cd ..
> ls


    Directory: C:\Users\zed\temp\stuff


Mode                LastWriteTime     Length Name
----                -------------     ------ ----
d----         12/17/2011    9:14 AM          things


> rmdir things
> cd ..
```

```
> ls

    Directory: C:\Users\zed\temp


Mode                 LastWriteTime        Length Name
----                 -------------        ------ ----
d----        12/17/2011   9:14 AM                stuff


> rmdir stuff
> pwd

Path
----
C:\Users\zed\temp


> cd ..
>
```

You Learned This

I'm now mixing up the commands, so make sure you type them exactly and pay attention. Every time you make a mistake, it's because you aren't paying attention. If you find yourself making many mistakes, then take a break or just quit for the day. You've always got tomorrow to try again.

In this example, you'll learn how to remove a directory. It's easy. You just go to the directory right above it, then type `rmdir <dir>`, replacing `<dir>` with the name of the directory to remove.

Do More

- Make 20 more directories and remove them all.

- Make a single path of directories that is 10 deep and remove them one at a time, just like I did above.

- If you try to remove a directory with contents, you will get an error. I'll show you how to remove these in later exercises.

Exercise 8: Move Around (pushd, popd)

In this exercise, you learn how to save your current location and go to a new location with pushd. You then learn how to return to the saved location with popd.

Do This

```
$ cd temp
$ mkdir -p i/like/icecream
$ pushd i/like/icecream
~/temp/i/like/icecream ~/temp
$ popd
~/temp
$ pwd
~/temp
$ pushd i/like
~/temp/i/like ~/temp
$ pwd
~/temp/i/like
$ pushd icecream
~/temp/i/like/icecream ~/temp/i/like ~/temp
$ pwd
~/temp/i/like/icecream
$ popd
~/temp/i/like ~/temp
$ pwd
~/temp/i/like
$ popd
~/temp
$ pushd i/like/icecream
~/temp/i/like/icecream ~/temp
$ pushd
~/temp ~/temp/i/like/icecream
$ pwd
~/temp
$ pushd
~/temp/i/like/icecream ~/temp
$ pwd
~/temp/i/like/icecream
$
```

```
> cd temp
> mkdir -p i/like/icecream


    Directory: C:\Users\zed\temp\i\like


Mode                LastWriteTime     Length Name
----                -------------     ------ ----
d----        12/20/2011  11:05 AM            icecream


> pushd i/like/icecream
```

```
> popd
> pwd

Path
----
C:\Users\zed\temp


> pushd i/like
> pwd

Path
----
C:\Users\zed\temp\i\like


> pushd icecream
> pwd

Path
----
C:\Users\zed\temp\i\like\icecream


> popd
> pwd

Path
----
C:\Users\zed\temp\i\like


> popd
>
```

You Learned This

You're getting into programmer territory with these commands, but they're so handy I have to teach them to you. These commands let you temporarily go to a different directory and then come back, easily switching between the two.

The pushd command takes your current directory and "pushes" it into a list for later; then it *changes* to another directory. It's like saying, "Save where I am, then go here."

The popd command takes the last directory you pushed and "pops" it off, taking you back there.

Finally, on Unix pushd, if you run it by itself with no arguments, will switch between your current directory and the last one you pushed. It's an easy way to switch between two directories. *This does not work in PowerShell.*

Do More

- Use these commands to move around directories all over your computer.

- Remove the i/like/icecream directories and make your own, then move around in them.

- Explain to yourself the output that pushd and popd will print out for you. Notice how it works like a stack?

- You already know this, but remember that mkdir -p will make an entire path even if all the directories don't exist. That's what I did very first for this exercise.

Exercise 9: Make Empty Files (Touch, New-Item)

In this exercise, you learn how to make an empty file using the touch (new-item on Windows) command.

Do This

```
$ cd temp
$ touch iamcool.txt
$ ls
iamcool.txt
$
```

```
> cd temp
> New-Item iamcool.txt -type file
> ls


    Directory: C:\Users\zed\temp


Mode                LastWriteTime     Length Name
----                -------------     ------ ----
-a---        12/17/2011    9:03 AM           iamcool.txt


>
```

You Learned This

You learned how to make an empty file. On Unix, touch does this, and it also changes the times on the file. I rarely use it for anything other than making empty files. On Windows, you don't have this command, so you learned how to use the New-Item command, which does the same thing but can also make new directories.

Do More

- **Unix.** Make a directory, change to it, and then make a file in it. Then change one level up and run the rmdir command in this directory. You *should* get an error. Try to understand why you got this error.

- **Windows.** Do the same thing, but you won't get an error. You'll get a prompt asking if you really want to remove the directory.

Exercise 10: Copy a File (cp)

In this exercise, you learn how to copy a file from one location to another with the cp command.

Do This

Exercise 10 Session

```
$ cd temp
$ cp iamcool.txt neat.txt
$ ls
iamcool.txt neat.txt
$ cp neat.txt awesome.txt
$ ls
awesome.txt iamcool.txt neat.txt
$ cp awesome.txt thefourthfile.txt
$ ls
awesome.txt  iamcool.txt  neat.txt  thefourthfile.txt
$ mkdir something
$ cp awesome.txt something/
$ ls
awesome.txt iamcool.txt  neat.txt  something  thefourthfile.txt
$ ls something/
awesome.txt
$ cp -r something newplace
$ ls newplace/
awesome.txt
$
```

Exercise 10 Windows Session

```
> cd temp
```

```
> cp iamcool.txt neat.txt
> ls


    Directory: C:\Users\zed\temp


Mode                LastWriteTime     Length Name
----                -------------     ------ ----
-a---        12/22/2011    4:49 PM          0 iamcool.txt
-a---        12/22/2011    4:49 PM          0 neat.txt


> cp neat.txt awesome.txt
> ls


    Directory: C:\Users\zed\temp


Mode                LastWriteTime     Length Name
----                -------------     ------ ----
-a---        12/22/2011    4:49 PM          0 awesome.txt
-a---        12/22/2011    4:49 PM          0 iamcool.txt
-a---        12/22/2011    4:49 PM          0 neat.txt


> cp awesome.txt thefourthfile.txt
> ls


    Directory: C:\Users\zed\temp


Mode                LastWriteTime     Length Name
----                -------------     ------ ----
-a---        12/22/2011    4:49 PM          0 awesome.txt
-a---        12/22/2011    4:49 PM          0 iamcool.txt
-a---        12/22/2011    4:49 PM          0 neat.txt
-a---        12/22/2011    4:49 PM          0 thefourthfile.txt


> mkdir something


    Directory: C:\Users\zed\temp


Mode                LastWriteTime     Length Name
----                -------------     ------ ----
d----        12/22/2011    4:52 PM            something


> cp awesome.txt something/
```

```
> ls
```

```
    Directory: C:\Users\zed\temp


Mode                LastWriteTime      Length Name
----                -------------      ------ ----
d----        12/22/2011    4:52 PM            something
-a---        12/22/2011    4:49 PM          0 awesome.txt
-a---        12/22/2011    4:49 PM          0 iamcool.txt
-a---        12/22/2011    4:49 PM          0 neat.txt
-a---        12/22/2011    4:49 PM          0 thefourthfile.txt


> ls something
```

```
    Directory: C:\Users\zed\temp\something


Mode                LastWriteTime      Length Name
----                -------------      ------ ----
-a---        12/22/2011    4:49 PM          0 awesome.txt


> cp -recurse something newplace
> ls newplace
```

```
    Directory: C:\Users\zed\temp\newplace


Mode                LastWriteTime      Length Name
----                -------------      ------ ----
-a---        12/22/2011    4:49 PM          0 awesome.txt


>
```

You Learned This

Now you can copy files. It's simple to just take a file and copy it to a new one. In this exercise, I also make a new directory and copy a file into that directory.

I'm going to tell you a secret about programmers and system administrators now. They are lazy. I'm lazy. My friends are lazy. That's why we use computers. We like to make computers do boring things for us. In the exercises so far, you have been typing repetitive boring commands so that you can learn them, but usually it's not like this. Usually if you find yourself doing something boring and repetitive, there's probably a programmer who has figured out how to make it easier. You just don't know about it.

The other thing about programmers is they aren't nearly as clever as you think. If you over think what to type, then you'll probably get it wrong. Instead, try to imagine what the name of a command is to you and try it. Chances are that it's a name or some abbreviation similar to what you thought it was. If you still can't figure it out intuitively, then ask around and search online. Hopefully it's not something really stupid like ROBOCOPY.

Do More

- Use the `cp  -r` command to copy more directories with files in them.

- Copy a file to your home directory or desktop.

- Find these files in your graphical user interface and open them in a text editor.

- Notice how sometimes I put a / (slash) at the end of a directory? That makes sure the file is really a directory, so if the directory doesn't exist, I'll get an error.

Exercise 11: Move a File (mv)

In this exercise, you learn how to move a file from one location to another, using the mv command.

Do This

Exercise 11 Session

```
$ cd temp
$ mv awesome.txt uncool.txt
$ ls
newplace        uncool.txt
$ mv newplace oldplace
$ ls
oldplace        uncool.txt
$ mv oldplace newplace
$ ls
newplace        uncool.txt
$
```

Exercise 11 Windows Session

```
> cd temp
> mv awesome.txt uncool.txt
> ls

    Directory: C:\Users\zed\temp
```

```
Mode                LastWriteTime        Length Name
----                -------------        ------ ----
d----     12/22/2011    4:52 PM                 newplace
d----     12/22/2011    4:52 PM                 something
-a---     12/22/2011    4:49 PM              0 iamcool.txt
-a---     12/22/2011    4:49 PM              0 neat.txt
-a---     12/22/2011    4:49 PM              0 thefourthfile.txt
-a---     12/22/2011    4:49 PM              0 uncool.txt


> mv newplace oldplace
> ls


    Directory: C:\Users\zed\temp


Mode                LastWriteTime        Length Name
----                -------------        ------ ----
d----     12/22/2011    4:52 PM                 oldplace
d----     12/22/2011    4:52 PM                 something
-a---     12/22/2011    4:49 PM              0 iamcool.txt
-a---     12/22/2011    4:49 PM              0 neat.txt
-a---     12/22/2011    4:49 PM              0 thefourthfile.txt
-a---     12/22/2011    4:49 PM              0 uncool.txt


> mv oldplace newplace
> ls newplace


    Directory: C:\Users\zed\temp\newplace


Mode                LastWriteTime        Length Name
----                -------------        ------ ----
-a---     12/22/2011    4:49 PM              0 awesome.txt


> ls


    Directory: C:\Users\zed\temp


Mode                LastWriteTime        Length Name
----                -------------        ------ ----
d----     12/22/2011    4:52 PM                 newplace
d----     12/22/2011    4:52 PM                 something
-a---     12/22/2011    4:49 PM              0 iamcool.txt
-a---     12/22/2011    4:49 PM              0 neat.txt
-a---     12/22/2011    4:49 PM              0 thefourthfile.txt
```

```
-a---          12/22/2011   4:49 PM         0 uncool.txt


>
```

You Learned This

Moving files or, rather, renaming them. It's easy: give the old name and the new name.

Do More

- Move a file in the newplace directory to another directory and then move it back.

Exercise 12: View a File (less, MORE)

To do this exercise, you're going to do some work using the commands you know so far. You'll also need a text editor that can make plain text (.txt) files. Here's what you do:

- Open your text editor and type some stuff into a new file. On OSX, this could be TextWrangler. On Windows, this might be Notepad++. On Linux, this could be gedit. Any editor will work.

- Save that file to your desktop and name it test.txt.

- In your shell, use the commands you know to *copy* this file to your temp directory that you've been working with.

Once you've done that, complete this exercise.

Do This

Exercise 12 Session

```
$ less test.txt
[displays file here]
$
```

That's it. To get out of less, just type q (as in quit).

Exercise 12 Windows Session

```
> more test.txt
[displays file here]
>
```

> **NOTE:** In the above output, I'm showing [displays file here] to "abbreviate" what that program shows. I'll do this when I mean to say, "Showing you the output of this program is too complex, so just insert what you see on your computer here and pretend I did show it to you." Your screen will not actually show this.

You Learned This

This is one way to look at the contents of a file. It's useful, because if the file has many lines, it will "page" so that only one screenful at a time is visible. In the Do More section, you'll play with this some more.

Do More

- Open your text file again and repeatedly copy-paste the text so that it's about 50–100 lines long.

- Copy it to your temp directory again so you can look at it.

- Now do the exercise again, but this time page through it. On Unix, you use the spacebar and w (the letter w) to go down and up. Arrow keys also work. On Windows, just hit the spacebar to page through.

- Look at some of the empty files you created too.

- The cp command will overwrite files that already exist so be careful copying files around.

Exercise 13: Stream a File (cat)

You're going to do some more setup for this one so you get used to making files in one program and then accessing them from the command line. With the same text editor from the last exercise, create another file named test2.txt, but this time save it directly to your temp directory.

Do This

Exercise 13 Session

```
$ less test2.txt
[displays file here]
$ cat test2.txt
I am a fun guy.
Don't you know why?
Because I make poems,
```

```
that make babies cry.
$ cat test.txt
Hi there this is cool.
$
```

```
> more test2.txt
[displays file here]
> cat test2.txt
I am a fun guy.
Don't you know why?
Because I make poems,
that make babies cry.
> cat test.txt
Hi there this is cool.
>
```

Remember that when I say [displays file here], I'm abbreviating the output of that command so I don't have to show you exactly everything.

You Learned This

Do you like my poem? Totally going to win a Nobel. Anyway, you already know the first command, and I'm just having you check that your file is there. Then you cat the file to the screen. This command just spews the whole file to the screen with no paging or stopping. To demonstrate that, I have you do this to the test.txt, which should just spew a bunch of lines from that exercise.

Do More

- Make a few more text files and work with cat.

- Unix: Try cat test.txt test2.txt and see what it does.

- Windows: Try cat test.txt,test2.txt and see what it does.

Exercise 14: Remove a File (rm)

In this exercise, you learn how to remove (delete) a file using the rm command.

Do This

```
$ cd temp
```

```
$ ls
uncool.txt  iamcool.txt  neat.txt  something  thefourthfile.txt
$ rm uncool.txt
$ ls
iamcool.txt  neat.txt  something  thefourthfile.txt
$ rm iamcool.txt neat.txt thefourthfile.txt
$ ls
something
$ cp -r something newplace
$
$ rm something/awesome.txt
$ rmdir something
$ rm -rf newplace
$ ls
$
```

Exercise 14 Windows Session

```
> cd temp
> ls
```

    Directory: C:\Users\zed\temp

Mode	LastWriteTime		Length	Name
d----	12/22/2011	4:52 PM		newplace
d----	12/22/2011	4:52 PM		something
-a---	12/22/2011	4:49 PM	0	iamcool.txt
-a---	12/22/2011	4:49 PM	0	neat.txt
-a---	12/22/2011	4:49 PM	0	thefourthfile.txt
-a---	12/22/2011	4:49 PM	0	uncool.txt

```
> rm uncool.txt
> ls
```

    Directory: C:\Users\zed\temp

Mode	LastWriteTime		Length	Name
d----	12/22/2011	4:52 PM		newplace
d----	12/22/2011	4:52 PM		something
-a---	12/22/2011	4:49 PM	0	iamcool.txt
-a---	12/22/2011	4:49 PM	0	neat.txt
-a---	12/22/2011	4:49 PM	0	thefourthfile.txt

```
> rm iamcool.txt
> rm neat.txt
```

```
> rm thefourthfile.txt
> ls
```

Directory: C:\Users\zed\temp

Mode	LastWriteTime		Length	Name
----	------------		------	----
d----	12/22/2011	4:52 PM		newplace
d----	12/22/2011	4:52 PM		something


```
> cp -r something newplace
> rm something/awesome.txt
> rmdir something
> rm -r newplace
> ls
>
```

You Learned This

Here we clean up the files from the last exercise. Remember when I had you try to `rmdir` on a directory with something in it? Well, that failed because you can't remove a directory with files in it. To do that, you have to remove the file or recursively delete all its contents. That's what you did at the end of this.

Do More

- Clean up everything in temp from all the exercises so far.

- Write in your notebook to be careful when running recursive remove on files.

Exercise 15: Exit Your Terminal (exit)

Do This

Exercise 23 Session

```
$ exit
```

Exercise 23 Windows Session

```
> exit
```

You Learned This

Your final exercise is how to exit your Terminal. Again, this is very easy, but I'm going to have you do more.

Do More

For your last set of exercises, I'm going to have you use the help system to look up a set of commands you should research and learn how to use on your own.

Here's the list for Unix:

- xargs
- sudo
- chmod
- chown

For Windows, look up these things:

- forfiles
- runas
- attrib
- icacls

Find out what these are, play with them, and then add them to your index cards.

Command Line Next Steps

You have completed the crash course. At this point, you should be a barely capable shell user. There's a whole huge list of tricks and key sequences you don't know yet, and I'm going to give you a few final places to go research more.

Unix Bash References

The shell you've been using is called Bash. It's not the greatest shell but it's everywhere and has a lot of features, so it's a good start. Here's a short list of links about Bash you should go read:

Bash Cheat Sheet   http://cli.learncodethehardway.org/bash_cheat_sheet.pdf created by Raphael (http://freeworld.posterous.com/65140847) and CC licensed.

Reference Manual   http://www.gnu.org/software/bash/manual/bashref.html

PowerShell References

On Windows, there's really only PowerShell. Here's a list of useful links for you related to PowerShell:

Owner's Manual   http://technet.microsoft.com/en-us/library/ee221100.aspx

Cheat Sheet   http://www.microsoft.com/download/en/details.aspx?displaylang=en&id=7097

Master PowerShell   http://powershell.com/cs/blogs/ebook/default.aspx

Index

DVD-ROM Warranty

Addison-Wesley warrants the enclosed DVD-ROM be free of defects in materials and faulty work-manship under normal use for a period of ninety days after purchase (when purchased new). If a defect is discovered in the DVD-ROM during this warranty period, a replacement DVD-ROM can be obtained at no charge by sending the defective DVD-ROM, postage prepaid, with proof of purchase to:

Disc Exchange
Addison-Wesley
Pearson Technology Group
75 Arlington Street, Suite 300
Boston, MA 02116

Email: disc.exchange@pearson.com

Addison-Wesley makes no warranty or representation, either expressed or implied, with respect to this software, its quality, performance, merchantability, or fitness for a particular purpose. In no event will Addison-Wesley, its distributors, or dealers be liable for direct, indirect, special, inci-dental, or consequential damages arising out of the use or inability to use the software. The exclu-sion of implied warranties is not permitted in some states. Therefore, the above exclusion may not apply to you. This warranty provides you with specific legal rights. There may be other rights that you may have that vary from state to state. The contents of this DVD-ROM are intended for personal use only.

More information and updates are available at:

informit.com/aw

 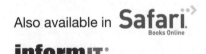